The
Reality
of **Illusion**

The
Reality
of Illusion

An Ecological Approach to Cognitive Film Theory

Joseph D. Anderson

Southern Illinois University Press
Carbondale and Edwardsville

Library of Congress Cataloging-in-Publication Data

Anderson, Joseph, 1940–
The reality of illusion : an ecological approach to
cognitive film theory / Joseph D. Anderson.
p. cm.
Includes bibliographical references and index.
1. Motion picture audiences—Psychology.
2. Motion pictures—Psychological aspects. I. Title.
PN1995.9.A8A5 1996
791.43'01'3—dc20   94-48221
ISBN 0-8093-2196-3 (pbk.)   CIP

To
Sam Becker
and **Harold Bechtoldt**

Contents

Preparation for this book began twenty-five years ago when, as a graduate student at the University of Iowa, I discovered that film history, theory, and criticism were constituted pretty much the same as literary history, theory, and criticism, except that in the former a group of motion pictures was substituted for a body of literature. While such an approach might suffice for history and criticism, it seemed to me woefully ineffectual for film theory. I knew of no literary theory capable of addressing the interaction between a spectator and the series of images and sounds that constitute a motion picture. I was fascinated by the special power of the motion picture, for as a filmmaker, I had learned to work some of the magic, but I had no idea how the magic worked.

In his role as department chairman, Sam Becker listened patiently as I laid out my misgivings, and he suggested that perhaps the kinds of questions I was asking might be addressed by experimental research in perception and cognition. It was with his blessing that I set out to find someone in the psychology department familiar with such matters. And as luck would have it, in the bowels of Spence Laboratory, I found a perception specialist, Harold Bechtoldt. I promptly asked him to explain to me how we perceive images and sounds, and it is my great fortune that he began an explanation that held me entranced for the next three years. I pursued an interdepartmental degree under the direction of both Sam and Harold, and it is to them that I dedicate this book as a token payment on the great debt I owe them.

As a young faculty member in the Department of Communication Arts at the University of Wisconsin, I taught motion picture production and film theory and set up a laboratory to conduct research on the perception of motion pictures. The theory course was entitled "Psychophysics and

Cinema," and in it, I attempted to bring some of the research in experimental psychology to bear upon problems of film-making and film viewing. In doing so, I learned two very important things—first, that it was not easy to match research findings in perception and cognition with problems of film production and spectatorship. I needed some sort of theoretical structure that would encompass both. What I needed was a metatheory, a theory to deal with other theories, and I began to find such a metatheory in the writings of J. J. and Eleanor Gibson. Second, I discovered that my students were delighted at a direct, research-based approach to film study. They seemed genuinely enthusiastic about an approach to film theory that confronted the medium directly and asked how motion pictures interact with spectators and how spectators process motion pictures.

A few years ago, I was invited back to the University of Iowa as a guest professor. I had been away from academia working in the motion picture industry for a decade, but when I offered a course in cognitive film theory, I discovered that students were again enthusiastic about addressing the basic questions of film theory from the perspective of the way the medium actually works rather than as an endless discussion of position taking. To paraphrase E. H. Gombrich, my students are much more interested in what one has found out than in where one stands.[1]

My intention is to bring the reader up to date on what I have found out about the application of cognitive science to the field of film theory. Specifically, I have selected from both basic and recent work in a variety of disciplines (such as visual perception, neurophysiology, cognitive psychology, social psychology, developmental psychology, and anthropology) fundamental concepts as well as specific findings that are pertinent to the issues of film production and spectatorship.

---

1. E. H. Gombrich, "Representation and Misrepresentation," *Critical Inquiry* 11, 2 (Dec. 1984): 199.

The book is organized as an explanation of how motion pictures interact with the human mind. Of course, my explanation is incomplete but I hope suggestive. My goal is to call attention to and explain actual phenomena as thoroughly as possible rather than to perfect arguments.

I have written this book for my students here at the University of Kansas, for students everywhere who are now in the process of asking fundamental questions about the nature of film, and for those who will be asking such questions as this decade metamorphoses into a new century. And though I do not expect to convert many of the current generation who have built their careers upon the film theory of the past fifteen or twenty years, I hope that film scholars who have not heretofore considered a cognitive film theory, let alone an ecological one, will read with an open mind.

Perhaps I should note that there are a few instances in the book where I have chosen to use the pronouns *he* and *his* rather than *he or she* and *his or her*, or alternately *they* and *their*. These are instances in which it was necessary to explain the responses or processes of not a group but an individual, making the use of a singular pronoun necessary. In these cases, the repeated use of *he or she* or *his or her* was intrusive and distracted from the explanation. When confronted with these circumstances, I chose to use the masculine pronoun because there has been a long tradition in the English language for use of the masculine pronoun as gender inclusive. My use of the masculine pronoun in these instances is so intended.

Finally, it is apparent to me that the people who make movies know a great deal about how movies actually work in the minds of viewers. Their insights have usually been gained by trial and error, and they may find value in a theoretical framework that can hold together all that they have discovered. As a filmmaker, I craved such an overall organizing structure. I hope filmmakers as well as film scholars will find in an ecological approach to cognitive film theory a means of uniting the information they already have with new findings from ongoing experimental research.

The general organization of the book is to relate filmic structures to human capacities for interacting with those structures. Specifically, the first three chapters are intended to provide an ecological overview, to place contemporary motion picture spectators in an evolutionary context so that our overall capacity to understand and enjoy a motion picture, which is largely taken for granted, can be seen as the accumulation of many discrete capacities acquired through millions of years of evolutionary development. Chapter 4 lays out some very specific problems long associated with motion picture viewing and offers some alternative explanations based on research findings in cognitive science.

Though contemporary motion pictures are bimodal in their construction, most of our discussion and examples are taken from research findings in *visual* processing. The decision to do so was based on a desire to keep the discussion focused and moving forward. Actually, a great deal of research has been done on the processing of sound, and a wealth of information is available in the literature. Chapter 5 is an attempt to acknowledge some of the rich interaction of visual and aural processing and to demonstrate some of the ways this interaction is recognized and exploited in motion pictures. Chapters 6 through 9 concentrate on specific aspects of filmic structure: continuity, diegesis, character, and narrative, and describe how each of these can exist as a component of filmic structure because they exploit the cache of human capacities piled up in the struggle for survival. In the final chapter, I attempt to show how the human capacity for framing an activity such as play can interact with our potential for illusion and surrogacy as we participate in the fictional world of a motion picture.

Acknowledgments

Many of the debts I owe are so long-standing that I can list them only upon some imaginary ledger, for they are by now beyond any hope of repayment. But, of course, the treasures my teachers bestowed upon me were generously offered as gifts and were intended to place no burden of debt—yet I still feel a great weight. To Sam Becker, Harold Bechtoldt, John Bowers, James Braddock, Ray Fielding, Bob Knipschild, John Kuiper, Armin Scheler, and John Winnie, I make substantial entries in the ledger.

I am grateful to Dudley Andrew and Franklin Miller for inviting me to the University of Iowa as a visiting professor, in which capacity I prepared the set of lectures that eventually informed this book. My colleagues here at the University of Kansas have also offered unflagging support even when they thought me wrongheaded in my approach. For this generous vote of confidence and for illuminating discussions of contemporary cultural theory, I am grateful to Chuck Berg and to John Gronbeck-Tedesco, and I am especially grateful to Ed Small for his continuing insights into the many issues of film theory. My long time friend and colleague David Bordwell bears a large responsibility, along with Noel Carroll and Edward Branigan, for encouraging me to complete and publish this book. I should hasten to add, however, that they are in no way responsible for any shortcomings that may be discerned in the work; any errors or omissions are my own.

I am indebted to Megan Gannon and Marilyn Heath for their work on the illustrations and the manuscript and to Barbara Anderson for her unwavering enthusiasm for the book and her untiring support for its author. Lastly, let me thank those students, in classes both at the University of Iowa and here at the University of Kansas, who have challenged my assertions, questioned my supporting evidence, and offered imaginative alternatives. By means of their lively debate, they have led me to strive for greater clarity with regard to the concepts presented in the following pages.

1
Introduction

The massive outer world has lost its weight, it has been freed from space, time, and causality, and it has been clothed in the forms of our own consciousness. The mind has triumphed over matter and the pictures roll on with the ease of musical tones. It is a superb enjoyment which no other art can furnish us.

—Hugo Munsterberg, *The Photoplay: A Psychological Study*

"Why does a movie seem so real? And why do the spokes of a wheel turn backward?" These are questions that many untutored film viewers ask in one form or another, but my interrogator at the moment was not untutored. He was, perhaps, unschooled in theories of film but well trained in the art of asking questions. He was, after all, an attorney.

As a movie viewer, he had no doubt many times been caught up in the enchantment of the world of the motion picture only to have the spell shattered by the intrusion of a stagecoach or carriage wheel that perversely rotated in the wrong direction. His lawyer's suspicions had been aroused. His sense of reality had been toyed with. He knew that something was not quite right. Now he had before him an "expert witness" from whom he would extract the truth.

I squirmed in my chair and perhaps failed to look him directly in the eye, for I knew that out of either naïveté or, worse yet, practiced lawyer's cunning, he had come upon a major inconsistency, a central paradox underlying the art of the motion picture—its capacity for realism and its denial of reality. A generation of film theorists before me had lined up to argue that the motion picture was *not* entirely realistic and therefore could take its place as a bona fide art. Others had argued that the value of the motion picture lay precisely in its capacity for realism. I knew that if I ventured in either direction, mountains of evidence could be weighed against me. Worse yet, he seemed to be asking about more than realism; he wanted an explanation of his experience of a motion picture. What could I say or do? I was trapped.

I took a sip of coffee and slowly looked my inquisitor in the eye. Fortunately, I was not testifying before a court of law but having a cup of coffee with my learned friend. Nevertheless, I responded as truthfully as I knew how. "They are illusions, both the sense of reality and the wheels that rotate in reverse."

My friend leaned against the back of his chair and lightly brushed his moustache with the tips of his fingers. "You have not answered my question," he said evenly. "You have merely given me the word *illusions*, a name, a category, not an explanation. A category is not an explanation. What is required is a reason, a cause, at least a relationship, perhaps a mechanism. If you answer 'illusions' to my question of why movies look so real and yet spoked wheels turn backward, then you must explain what illusions are and what they have to do with motion pictures."

I began searching through my pockets for some change for the waiter. "We had better adjourn this session," I said emphatically, fearing the answers to his questions would fill a book.

What makes the lawyer's tale worth telling is that although we live in a time when crime flourishes, minorities are oppressed, women are victimized, and evil abounds in the world (and these are things with which he is professionally familiar), he chooses to focus not on the overt content of particular motion pictures, but on the source of the power of the motion picture generically, power that he has no doubt witnessed by effect in the world at large, but more to the point, a power he has personally felt while sitting in the theater watching a movie. He wants to know why a motion picture gives him compelling reality in one moment and takes it back in the next. Is it something in the picture or something in him that provides this push-pull in and out of the world of the motion picture? In his unguided and perhaps naive search for an understanding of the great attractive force he feels tugging at him from the screen, he had focused upon the obvious, the interface between the film and the viewer, an area that professional film scholars have phobically avoided for almost a century. By a strange progression of events, the longer scholars have studied film, the farther they have moved from the interface between the film and the viewer and, it might be argued, from an understanding of the source of cinematic power.

There was no way my barrister friend could have known that he had innocently invaded the domain of film theory, which has existed almost as long as the motion picture itself and has for some time been distinguishable from its sister disciplines, film history and film criticism. If these two disciplines have concerned themselves with the events of film's emergence, with placing its development in the context of other events, with finding causes, and with interpreting and evaluating specific films and groups of films respectively, film theory has endeavored to answer the most fundamental questions as to the nature of film, questions relating to what film is and how it works. Over the last century, several film theories have been offered, usually setting forth one or more principles along with supporting arguments and proposed implications.

For the benefit of my learned friend and anyone else who may not have closely followed the progress of film theory throughout this century, I offer a thumbnail sketch with commentary of the history of film theory. The first film theorist, Hugo Munsterberg, came to Harvard in 1892 at the invitation of William James, not to be a film theorist of course, but to help set up a psychological laboratory. It was as one of the founders of American psychology that he wrote *The Photoplay: A Psychological Study*, published in 1916.[1]

Munsterberg was familiar with the empirical research being done across a broad spectrum of psychological areas. Much of it was being carried out in his own laboratory at Harvard. The tools of what would become the social sciences were being discovered, and they were being put to every conceivable task. The research of the day was a pragmatic enterprise dedicated to finding out how things work. Munsterberg brought this interest in practical problem solving along with his specific knowledge of the results of scientific experiments in psychology to the study of film. In doing so, he demonstrated that empirical investigation can illuminate our understanding of the motion picture. He concluded from his short but intense study of the interface between the film and the viewer that the motion picture is structured in a way that is analogous to the structuring processes of the mind. From such a principle, he was able to elaborate a complex and inclusive theory of film.

It was a stroke of luck for the field of film theory to have as its founder one of the most brilliant and educated men of the day. Specifically, the good fortune lay in that one of the very few people capable of analyzing the interface between the motion picture and the mind of the viewer chose to do so. He set film theory clearly on a path that would have confronted the basic questions about the nature and function of film in a direct and systematic way. Unfortunately, his was a path no one chose to follow.

Those film theorists writing during the first half of the century beginning with Munsterberg and concluding with André Bazin (including Soviet theorists Lev Kuleshov, V. I. Pudovkin, and Sergei Eisenstein, along with Rudolf Arnheim and Siegfried Kracauer) are usually considered together, and their work collectively referred to as classical film theory. Though they diverge greatly in their theories of film, these theorists are united both by their proximity in time and by a common interest in defining film as an art equal in status to the more traditional fine arts such as painting, dance, and theater.

The first wave of film theory was devoted to the defense

of film as art, and once film was successfully established as an art meriting the same attention as the other arts, the direction of film theory was pretty well set. Enthusiastic young filmmakers and cineasts in several countries sought to do for the cinema what had been done for the other fine arts: to define the medium's essential components (as art) and to analyze their manifestation in particular works in that medium.

Theorists as divergent in geography and viewpoint as Bazin in France and Eisenstein in the Soviet Union chose to dwell upon issues related to how a motion picture might best be structured in order to maximize those aspects of the medium they each believed best revealed its unique character. Eisenstein set forth a theory of montage informed by Hegel's principle of dialectics. He described the process of montage as the collision of two shots (or particular aspects of shots) as a dialectical clash of two material concepts, resulting in a third and totally new abstract concept. And André Bazin offered a theory of film consistent with the philosophical movement of phenomenology, which denied a split between mind and matter, between the self and the world. For Bazin, the film was neither a product of the mind nor a clash of concepts but rather a photochemical record of reality. Upon this central premise he built an intricate and subtle realist theory of film.

The *auteur theory* that grew out of the publication *Cahiers du Cinema* in the fifties also accentuated the focus on film as an art, asserting that if film is an art then the director is the film artist. By virtue of this logical construct, it became possible to analyze not only an individual work of film art, but to look at the whole of an author's *oeuvre* as in the study of literature, drama, and painting. The way was thus paved for film to enter the academy in the full humanist tradition.

In the decades of the sixties and seventies, a number of film scholars, most notably Christian Metz, held that film was more than an art, that it was a language, and they based their film theory upon the linguistic theory of Ferdinand de Saussure. From such a perspective, they set out to develop a semiotics of film, to see film as a language or at least language-like and to identify its components. In semiotics, there was hope of answering the question of what film is (a system of signification) and to come to know how it works in a thorough and disciplined way.

But the optimism of classical and early semiotic film theory was soon supplanted by what must seem to the noninitiate as a most bizarre program derived from a marshaling of Freudian psychoanalysis in support of an academic strain of Marxism. The theory was an admixture of the neo-Marxism of Louis Althusser and the neo-Freudianism of Jacques Lacan in which concepts from psychoanalysis were fused with Marxism and applied to film.[2] From this perspective, film in general, as well as a specific motion picture, was seen as a covert and perhaps unwitting instructor of political ideology. For example, movies from America in particular were believed to propagate the concealed assumptions of capitalism (which carried a negative value in the psychoanalytic/Marxist system). Film in general, and indeed any particular film, came to be seen as a patient symptomatic of a sick society. Desires systematically repressed by the ruling elite could be brought to the surface and revealed, thus exposing the social disease. The film became the patient, and the film theorist took on the role of psychoanalyst. In time, feminist film theory came to occupy a section of the larger purchase of psychoanalytic/Marxist theory and tended to see film as an instrument of oppression and victimization. The role of the film theorist became that of exposing hidden agendas of power embodied in the films themselves.

In recent years, film studies, along with the arts and humanities collectively, has fallen into an attitude characterized as postmodernism, an attitude that has tended to revel in the eclectic, to advocate a revisionist view of history, and to retain a fascination with the revealing of things hidden. I use the word *attitude* rather than *theory* because while postmodernism appears to encompass many positions it is not itself a theory; it does not set forth a general principle; it is not a related body of facts. It is not even a hypothesis. It can be defined only by what it is not: it is not modernism, it is not science, and though it embraces eclecticism, it is none of the historical entities from which it pilfers. The attitude is one of self-absorption, and the perspective is elitist. There is the not-so-hidden assumption of a kind of worldliness, of a sophisticated cynicism on the part of initiates. Any view that is nonreflexive or nonironic is characterized as naive.

An apparent advantage to writing from this perspective is that film writers may feel free to appropriate the language of psychoanalysis, Marxism, or any pop culture movement or special interest cause, without assuming responsibility for their theoretical imperatives. Such writers may claim adherence to no theory at all. From such a perspective, film is seen merely as a vehicle for revealing problems of social conflict and authority. Postmodernists look *through* the medium of film and discuss its overt content (or perhaps what they see as its *covert* content). To the extent that they concern themselves with the medium, they are interested in it only as a purveyor of ideology. In the postmodernist era, there is no need to ask what film is or how it works. There is no need to pursue an understanding of the nature of film *qua* film. There is no need for film theory.

In its inherent nihilism, its self-concious quoting of the recent past, and its position in time at the end of both a century and an era, today's postmodernism has much in common with the mannerism that followed the Italian Renaissance and saw the sixteenth century to a close. If the analogy holds, there is hope for the future, for as the sixteenth century ended, the disillusionment of mannerism gave way to a new surge of the human spirit expressed in the art of Bernini and Rembrandt and the science of Galileo and Newton.

Actually, a life-affirming, reality-embracing revolution is already under way that offers a refreshing alternative to the effete cynicism of the postmodernist era. Scholars from such diverse fields as perceptual and cognitive psychology, linguistics, artificial intelligence, neurophysiology, and anthropology, who have confidence in the scientific method and an interest in understanding the workings of the human mind, are sharing information in pursuit of their common goal. They have spawned what has been called the cognitive revolution.

By the mid-eighties, a few courageous film theorists suggested that cognitive science might be a more productive path than the then-pervasive, psychoanalytic/Marxist approach to film study. Notably, David Bordwell in *Narration in the Fiction Film* suggested, among other things, that a film spectator might be *cued* by a film rather than *positioned* by it. And Noel Carroll in *Mystifying Movies* argued in detail that existing film theories served more to mystify than to explain the workings of motion pictures.[3]

In spite of science's unparalleled success in explaining the workings of the universe, the efforts of film theorists to apply the methods and findings of cognitive science to the issues of film studies have not met with unanimous approval from film scholars. Many have rejected not only the special thrust of cognitive science but science outright. Indeed, some are apparently fixed in the position that science is but another set of conventions, that its claim to special status is no greater than could be made by any culture for its religion or institutions, that science is no more than a tool of cultural imperialism with which Western culture attempts to maintain its dominance over the rest of the world. Though such a view apparently has a certain surface appeal, in order to maintain such notions advocates must somehow be willing to deny either the existence of reality itself or the possibility of knowing it.

Admittedly, the course of science has not been a straight path of progress. It has taken twists and turns and has sometimes backtracked. As Karl Popper has observed, it is, after all, a human endeavor like all human endeavors, albeit a special one.

The history of science, like the history of all human ideas, is a history of irresponsible dreams, of obstinacy, and of error. But science is one of the very few

human activities—perhaps the only one—in which
errors are systematically criticized and fairly often,
in time, corrected. This is why we can say that, in
science, we often learn from our mistakes, and why
we can speak clearly and sensibly about making
progress there. In most other fields of human endeavor there is change, but rarely progress.[4]

That science *can* be said to progress is part of its claim to
a special category among human enterprises. Science is built
upon the assumption that there is a physical world and that
it can be known by observation. Science proceeds by the formation of hypotheses about the world that are then tested.
The tests are required to be open and repeatable, and results
are continually questioned and reevaluated. It is the special-
ness of science, its uniqueness among human endeavors, however, that some film scholars have refused to grant. This is
not the place for a full exposition of the argument, but the
fact that film scholars took such a position for ten to fifteen
years left film study in the predicament in which we found
it at the beginning of this decade. In the absence of any criteria
for establishing the relative accuracy of a given theory, we
were left with what E. H. Gombrich has called *conventionalism*,
an attitude that counts all theories as equally valid, all signs
as conventional, all expectations as solely culturally determined, a "manifestly absurd relativism."[5]
    It is against such a backdrop of almost a century of film
theory ranging from the brilliantly creative to the totally absurd that I must attempt to explain to my friend why movies
seem so real. But my task is made much easier by the work
of cognitive film theorists and cognitive scientists. I shall not
repeat the work of my colleagues Bordwell and Carroll, who
freed film theory from the chokehold of the psychoana-
lytic/Marxist paradigm in the eighties and replaced it with
the perspective of cognitive science, which though not yet
universally accepted by film scholars is now firmly in place.
In the following pages, I shall take for granted the assump-

tions and methods of science in general and cognitive science in particular. My efforts will be directed toward placing cognitive science in a relationship to the film medium, and I shall describe a metatheory that can encompass both. I call this metatheory *ecological* because it attempts to place film production and spectatorship in a natural context. That is, the perception and comprehension of motion pictures is regarded as a subset of perception and comprehension in general, and the workings of the perceptual systems and the mind of the spectator are viewed in the context of their evolutionary development.

I shall simply begin at the beginning. For the motion picture, the beginning is the interface between a spectator and sounds and images on a screen. No detail of this interface can be responsibly ignored. When viewers sit before a theater or video screen to watch a movie, they face a sequence of images and sounds. The precise nature of the sequence is neither arbitrary nor random, but of a most carefully crafted order. The makers of the movie have often spent many months and millions of dollars to achieve perfection of individual elements and overall form.

The particular way a motion picture is crafted, those elements often referred to collectively as *style* have, particularly in the United States, developed in the direction of *accessibility*. Hugo Munsterberg in 1915 predicted that film would become the domain of the psychologist.[6] It has instead become the province of the entrepreneur. From the beginning, American films were subject to the contingencies of the free enterprise system; capital was raised and the picture was produced and then exhibited to viewers for the price of a ticket. For each picture, the success or failure of the entire venture was in the hands of the thousands of individual consumers who either purchased a ticket or did not. If a particular motion picture failed to sell enough tickets to return a profit to the investors, its producer and/or director was not likely to get the opportunity to make another picture. That is the way the system worked as the so-called *Hollywood style* developed in the second, third, and fourth decades of the twentieth century, and that is the way it works today. Such a system caused producers of motion pictures to make movies that appealed to a wider and wider audience. And that appeal is largely measured by the film's accessibility. That is to say that individual moviegoers are more apt to buy tickets to movies that are accessible to them, accessible in the most fundamental ways, such as whether it is possible to comprehend the fictional events that occur on the screen and to follow the basic story line. Apart from the obvious problem of language differences, which can be largely overcome with subtitles or dubbing, problems of accessibility are problems of perception. And though few if any of them had training in perceptual psychology, filmmakers in Hollywood proceeded to discover how to make their products accessible to individuals across economic and class boundaries and across national and cultural boundaries as well. A number of rules of thumb developed: that every shot should advance the story line, that actors should avoid broad gestures and never look directly into the lens, that there should be a change of camera angle and image size from one shot to the next, that the camera should be kept on one side of the action (the 180-degree rule), that the fictional world of the movie should never be intruded upon by the workers and equipment involved in its construction, and that the story should be told in action rather than words whenever possible. These rules were followed because they tended to make the events of the picture understandable to the individual spectator. For reasons both obvious and profound, following these rules made the picture accessible to a wider audience. Motion pictures made by these rules were generally thought to be more realistic, and indeed they were, as we shall discover in the following pages. Purely by trial and error, the moneymen, the technicians, and the artists who made up the American film industry succeeded in developing a style of filmmaking that was potentially accessible to every human being on earth.

Whatever its shortcomings, the classical Hollywood style became more universally accessible than any of its competitors, and it remains so today.

Let me note that accessibility is of theoretical and not political interest here. My purpose is not to argue for a privileged status for the classical Hollywood style, but to point out that the problem of accessibility in a motion picture is not merely a matter of culture. It is more fundamentally a matter of perception.

It is readily apparent that the motion picture/viewer interface is not equally balanced, for while a motion picture is created specifically for the viewer, the viewer was not created for watching motion pictures. The implications of the imbalance, however, are not so easy to grasp. It may be helpful to draw an analogy. The motion picture can be thought of as a program. And it is more precisely a program than either a language or a mere set of stimuli. It is a very complex set of instructions utilizing images, actions, and sounds, a string of commands to attend to *this* now, in this light, from this angle, at this distance, and so forth, and to recall earlier sequences and anticipate future ones. The program cannot be run on a projector or a videotape machine. These devices have no capacity to interact with the instructions. The program can "run" only in the mind of the viewer.

The viewer can be thought of as a standard biological audio/video processor. The central processing unit, the brain along with its sensory modules, is standard. The same model with only minor variations is issued to everyone. The basic operating system is also standard and universal, for both the brain and its functions were created over 150 million years of mammalian evolution.

Filmmakers can be seen as programmers who develop programs to run on a computer that they do not understand and whose operating systems were designed for another purpose. Since the filmmakers/programmers do not understand the operating system, they are never sure exactly what will happen with any frame or sequence of their programs. They therefore proceed by trial and error. They follow certain filmic conventions and then go beyond them by guessing. They test the outcome (that is, how their programs will be handled in the minds of viewers) by becoming viewers themselves and running the program in their own minds. This might be considered a fairly risky procedure, because each human mind is a little different, different sub-routines may be initiated by the same instruction, and different meanings may result in each mind. But the filmmakers-turned-viewers are not proceeding completely recklessly and irresponsibly, because the "hardware" of the mind and most of the "software" is standard and universal.

Such an analogy between the human mind and a computer is useful to the extent that it serves to help us grasp the relationships between the cinematic apparatus, the filmmaker, and our own processing systems. It also points out just how different our mind is from present-day computers. Both are capable of computing functions of considerable complexity, but the computer that I now employ in writing this text is a serial, digital, highly programmable device; the mind is none of these things. It is, first of all, much more complex. The brain itself is very likely the most complex structure in the universe. (The structure and function of the brain may be so integrated that to speak of hardware and software even by analogy may be unjustified.) It processes in parallel as well as sequentially, and it frustrates most attempts at reprogramming. Yet the brain is not as good as the simplest commercial computer at carrying out tasks like keeping track of expenses or balancing checkbooks, and there is little one can do to change its capacity or procedures for calculation. But it is very good at guiding our movements in three dimensional space, so we do not bump into trees, fall into chasms, or lose our way in the countryside. And it is very good at precisely locating an object of prey in space and guiding our arm in the hurling of a stone or spear with deadly accuracy. The point is that by whatever device or analogy, we must understand that our brains and sensory systems, indeed our very consciousness, our sense of self, our mind in all its implications, is the present result of past evolution, and for most of the time during this evolution, when our capacities were being cruelly sorted by the processes of natural selection, the contingencies of existence were quite different from what they are today.

For example, the origins of the human visual system vastly predate the emergence of humans. To move about with speed and agility, and to hunt successfully, an animal needed accurate information about the location of things in space. By the time humans emerged, the visual system in mammals was pretty well defined, and its central organizing principle was *veridicality*. This is to say that an individual's perception of the world needed to be a very close approximation of that world. It had to be accurate enough to act upon because the consequences of error were severe. If a creature could not detect the presence of a potential predator, it could not take evasive action, and its chances of surviving long enough to reproduce were greatly diminished. If a predator were not correct about the location of prey in space, it would not be successful as a hunter. It would starve, its young offspring would starve, and its genes would never be passed on to succeeding generations. The cold, indifferent process of evolution selected for veridicality in the visual system, not through purpose, but through contingency.

An interesting paradox of human perception is that although perceptual development has tended toward veridicality, we at times perceive illusions. The simplest definition of an illusion is that it is a nonveridical perception. But it is a *wide-awake* nonveridical perception. If we are asleep we may dream, if we are drugged or deranged we may hallucinate, and if we fast and meditate we may have a vision, but illusions occur even when we are awake, sane, and skeptical. For example, in the three-dimensional illusion, we perceive depth, when in reality, there are but two slightly offset images projected simultaneously upon a flat screen. Such illusions are particularly revealing about our perceptual systems. Visual

illusions, like 3-D, result when the visual system, following
its own internal instructions, arrives at a percept that is in
error if compared to physical reality. That is, illusions occur
because the system follows its own internal rules even though
the resulting percept is in error. To perceptual psychologists,
and by extension to those of us who would understand motion
picture viewing, illusions are of special interest because they
reveal the rules according to which the perceptual system
functions, rules that are ordinarily invisible. By studying the
system when it makes an "error" we can see the rules exposed;
by studying the rules we gain a greater understanding of how
the human mind interacts with a motion picture.

The major thesis developed in the pages that follow is that
the motion picture, or the phenomenon of cinema, can best
be understood by utilizing the methods of science within an
ecological context. We are and always have been part of a
larger ecology. In this interlocking relationship with the larger
ecological setting, we developed, through eons of evolution,
elaborate and sophisticated capacities to gain information.
Today, we interact with the synthesized images and sounds
of a motion picture, but we have no new capacities for gaining
information from them. We have only the systems developed
in another time, in another context, for another purpose. We
must process the images from the glass-beaded screen and
sounds from the metal speakers with the same anatomical
structures and the same physiological processes with which
we process scenes and sounds from the natural world. To ask
how we process continuity and character and narrative in
motion pictures is to ask how the forces of evolution equipped
us to know where we are in space and time, to make rapid
judgments of character, and to narratize the events of our
existence. When we delve into research on these questions,
we quickly realize that our capacities exist within boundaries,
and seldom if ever can those boundaries be overridden by
transitory cultural fad or clever linguistic fabrication.

2
Toward an Ecology of Cinema

Cognitive science is not a discipline in itself but an informal consortium of researchers in several disciplines such as cognitive psychology, artificial intelligence, philosophy, linguistics, and neurophysiology who share information in an effort to understand the nature and processes of the human mind. And what has come to be called cognitive film theory is perhaps not a theory by a rigorous definition of the term, but an attempt by a growing number of film scholars to apply the thinking and research, now pouring forth in great volume from cognitive science, to the problems of film production and spectatorship. Cognitive scientists are actively delving into such areas as learning, attention, memory, reasoning, and problem solving. They are asking how we acquire new knowledge and retrieve past experiences and what it means to be consciously aware. Film theorists have realized that the questions cognitive scientists have asked about mental activities are similar to questions they themselves have asked about motion pictures, such as how specific sequences are comprehended and remembered, how attention is shifted from one part of a scene to another, and how problem solving and reasoning are engaged in narrative. As cognitive scientists begin to understand various aspects of the workings of the human mind, film theorists begin to understand aspects of film viewing that were previously incomprehensible and mysterious to them. What an ecological approach offers is an overview, a way of stepping back from, and viewing as a whole, this very powerful set of assumptions, principles, and research findings derived from cognitive science that is being called cognitive film theory.

The term *ecological* implies an interdependence between elements of a larger system. Gregory Bateson, for instance, employed the term in his 1971 book *Steps Toward an Ecology of Mind*. Bateson placed ideas in an ecological context: "The questions which the book raises are ecological: How do ideas interact? Is there some sort of natural selection which determines the survival of some ideas and the extinction or death of others? What sort of economics limits the multiplicity of ideas in a given region of mind? What are the necessary conditions for stability (or survival) of such a system or subsystem?"[1] Though his emphasis was on the cultural context of ideas, it is apparent in the questions he posed that as the son of an eminent biologist and geneticist and as one concerned with "anthropology, psychiatry, biological evolution and genetics, and the new epistemology which comes out of systems theory and ecology,"[2] Bateson was acutely aware of the biological basis of all human endeavors.

So too was J. J. Gibson when he wrote *The Ecological Approach to Visual Perception* (1979). Gibson focused not on the ecology of ideas as ideas but the ecology of human perception, and his approach is overtly biological. As James Cutting has observed: "The underlying appeal of Gibson is to the ecology of the perceiver. But it is a particular ecology, deeply and fundamentally biological."[3] The ecological approach to film theory presented in the following pages rests, at its base, upon perception. That is, it is a perceptually based theory rather than a linguistically or politically based theory, and it begins with Gibson's ecological theory of perception.

Gibson realized that all human capacities for perceiving our world are rooted in our unique biological evolution as a species. Each capacity is particularly tailored to fit our biological niche at the time of its development. And to this day, for humans, the sensory perspective remains that of a creature walking around on the ground. The "earth-air interface," Gibson writes, is "the most important of all surfaces for terrestrial animals. This is the *ground*. It is the ground of their perception and behavior, both literally and figuratively. It is their surface of support."[4]

This fact impressed itself upon Gibson early in his career. As a young psychologist during World War II, Gibson was given the task of helping pilots fly and land airplanes. He quickly discovered that his training in psychology had not prepared him adequately. What he had been taught had come largely from experiments in visual perception carried out in laboratories, usually with subjects' heads held rigid and their eyes fixed upon a point. While much had been learned in this way about the physics of light and vision, there was very little to help one understand how a pilot might actually use his sense of vision to increase his chances of landing an airplane safely. Gibson realized the major difference was that airplane pilots were not sitting rigidly in a laboratory but were moving rapidly through the air above the ground; their problem was to make sense of a visual world rushing past them at astonishing speeds. Gibson understood that perception was profoundly connected to one's relationship to one's environment. But a theory of perception based upon a creature's interaction with an environment did not find easy acceptance in Gibson's day, nor has it found total acceptance today. Part of the problem was, and is, that such a theory goes against a long tradition of thinking about perception that originated with Hermann Ludwig Ferdinand Von Helmholtz.

Born in Potsdam, Germany, in the first quarter of the nineteenth century, Helmholtz achieved fame for measuring the rate at which a signal is propagated along a nerve path. His studies of the visual and the auditory systems taught him that sensory signals travel rather slowly and that they are processed by the brain even more slowly. He hypothesized that a great deal of processing occurred in all that time and that the sensory signals had meaning only in relation to associations built up by learning. For him, perception was definitely learned, but not necessarily conscious. It was a process of "unconscious inference."

The mainstream of perceptual psychology since Helmholtz has held that "our sensory receptors analyse the energies provided by the physical world into independent, simple, but unnoticeable sensations, and the world teaches us to perceive those objects and events."[5] Perceptions are somehow "constructed" from impoverished sensations, presumably through a process of unconscious inference.

Although finding no fault with Helmholtz's description of the basic physiology, Gibson rejected both the idea of construction and that of unconscious inference. He found the notion of inference, conscious or not, unpalatable. He questioned who was making the inference and felt that the concept of inference led to an infinite regress. He was fond of saying that there is no homunculus, no little green man in the brain making judgments or looking at pictures. For Gibson perception was direct; it needed neither mediation nor interpretation. It is this concept of direct perception in Gibson's ecological approach that has caused the most controversy. The schism between Gibson's theory of perception and that of traditional perceptual psychology runs right along the boundary between direct perception and mediated perception, and it becomes an open chasm over the notion of representation.[6]

Considerable confusion continues to surround the use of the term *representation*. In the field of film theory, even cognitive film theory, the term has been used to describe the motion picture as a consciously constructed, two-dimensional, man-made artifact. And indeed, the motion picture is such a construction. (Though I hasten to add that its status as a construction or representation does not preclude the motion picture from being an illusion or functioning as surrogate reality.) It is in this sense of acknowledging the representational status of a motion picture that Gibson would refer to the perception of film as "perception at second hand."[7] If this were the only sense in which the term were used I would gladly refer to film as a representation. Other uses, misuses, and misconceptions, however, abound.

In the fields of perceptual and cognitive psychology, for instance, *representation* is often used to refer to an internal representation, a kind of mental image created out of raw sensory material in the process of perception. Such a concept has no place in an ecological theory. Moreover, the term *representation* is often not clearly defined, and it is not used consistently even in the literature of perception. As perceptual psychologists Vicki Bruce and Patrick Green have noted, the term

> is used to refer to any symbolic description of the world—whether this is the world as it has been in the past (as in stored 'memories'), as it is now (the 2-1/2 D sketch or structural descriptions), or as it might be in the future (as in certain kinds of imagery). It is also used by "connectionist" theorists to refer to non-symbolic patterns of activation in simple networks, which, nevertheless *represent* some object, feature, distance or other property of the surroundings.[8]

When used in the latter sense, little conflict exists between a concept of representation and an ecological approach to perception. And it is possible to interpret some of the computational theories (even those that are avowedly representational) as providing a series of algorithms that describe the process taking place in ecological perception.

The first use of the term noted by Bruce and Green—to denote a symbolic description of the world as it has been in the past—points to yet another level of the representation debate. These representations are types of long-term memories that allow individuals to reconstruct spatial layouts of places seen sometime in the past; they have sometimes been called "cognitive maps." The problem presented for ecological perception is the definition of these representations as *symbolic* entities. Ulric Neisser succinctly summarized the issue:

> Spatial knowledge is often described as if it depended on mental representations called "cognitive maps," but this usage may take too much for granted. For one thing, it tends to bypass the more difficult questions; any aspect of spatial memory can be explained

by postulating a corresponding property of the map. It also suggests that a single coherent representation underlies all forms of spatial orientation—something that is unlikely to be the case.[9]

Gibson preferred to discuss this kind of behavior in the context of an observer's orientation to the environment and denied the need for "mapping" of any sort:

> To go from one place to another involves the opening up of the vista ahead and closing in of the vista behind. . . . When the vistas have been put in order by exploratory locomotion, the invariant structure of the house, the town or the whole habitat will be apprehended. . . . One is [then] oriented to the environment. It is not so much having a bird's-eye view of the terrain as it is being everywhere at once. The getting of a bird's-eye view is helpful in becoming oriented, and the explorer will look down from a high place if possible. . . . But orientation to goals behind the walls, beyond the trees, and over the hill is not just a looking-down-on, and it is certainly not the having of a map, not even a "cognitive" map supposed to exist in the mind instead of on paper. A map is a useful artifact when the hiker is lost, but it is a mistake to confuse the artifact with the psychological state the artifact promotes. . . . To the extent that one has moved from place to place, from vista to vista, one can stand still in one place and see where one is, which means where one is relative to where one might be. One does not need a map with a circle on it labeled, "You are here."[10]

This kind of orientation to one's environment, the nonsymbolic sense of a "cognitive map," if you will, tells us a great deal about one's orientation to the diegetic world of a motion picture, and the implications of that process pertain specifically to the selection of editing patterns in the narrative film. (These matters are discussed at length in chap. 6.)

Because of the existing muddle regarding the concept of representation, both in film and in perception, and because I do not wish to be understood to be referring to a symbolic mental representation constructed in the process of perception, I shall refrain from using the term.

The argument over representation concerns the larger questions of mediation in perception, whether it is necessary to form a mental representation of the object/event in the world in order to perceive it. The details of the debate between supporters of the two different paradigms for perception are outside the focus of this book, but it is my feeling that in addition to making intuitive sense, Gibson's ecological approach, when applied to cognitive film theory, affords us a new and promising way of studying film viewing. His approach helps to define the interface between film and viewer, not in terms of stimuli and sensations nor as cues for constructing meanings, but in terms of the meanings inherent in the very interaction of a creature with its environment—or more specifically the interaction of a creature with its *surrogate* environment. Indeed our perceptual systems developed in the direction of allowing us to interact more effectively with the world, and we interact with a motion picture in many of the same ways that we interact with the world.

We would therefore be well advised to study the ways in which the perceptual systems are employed by an organism interacting with its evironment. Only then can we come to appreciate how biological organisms such as ourselves have developed sensitivities to diverse aspects of the physical world: electromagnetic radiations, molecular disturbances in the air, the chemical makeups of gases and plants, and the characteristics of surfaces. And only by appreciating that we developed complex sensory systems that extract information from the environment by sensing patterns in these physical phenomena, can we begin to understand how consciously constructed man-made patterns such as those of a motion picture can constitute information for those sensory systems.

An Evolutionary Perspective

The theory accounting for how our perceptual systems, indeed all biological systems, developed was set forth by Charles Darwin in his *Origin of Species* in 1859, and the explosion of knowledge in the fields of genetics and molecular biology in our own time has only validated his basic concepts. Darwin's theory of evolution still underpins biological science today.[11]

The idea of plants and animals changing over time from one form into another was fairly well accepted in scientific circles by the time Darwin's work was published; indeed, Jean Baptiste de Lamarck had already offered a theory of evolution some fifty years earlier.[12] He proposed, among other things, that organisms have a built-in drive toward perfection and that acquired characteristics can be passed on to offspring.

But Darwin offered a very different idea: no grand plan, no drive toward perfection, and no inheritance of acquired characteristics. He proposed instead the principles of *diversity* and *natural selection*. By diversity he meant that in any given population individuals are not exactly alike; they vary from each other. He had observed the phenomenon during his five-year voyage to the Galapagos Islands, where he had been provided the opportunity to study long isolated populations of various species, and his observations led him to believe that the small differences between individuals in a species were heritable.

His choice of the term *natural selection* is purposely set in contrast to *artificial selection*, which was widely practiced in the breeding of domestic animals. Animal breeders of the day, including Darwin's father, selected certain individuals from their flocks or herds for breeding because they expressed desirable characteristics, such as a sheep with longer wool or a cow with a greater capacity to give milk. Darwin's great insight was that nature too selected some individuals to survive and have offspring. The principle he articulated was that the environment "selects" those individuals who, in their differences (usually very slight), are the most suited to it—those, for instance, who can survive the climate, catch and digest the available food, secure protection from predators, and find a mate. Diversity turns out to be a matter of chance and natural selection a matter of contingency.

It was by these same prinicples—diversity and natural selection—that the human perceptual systems developed. From the very beginning, we might ask, what was "selected" for? What constituted adaptation with regard to the sensory system? Ultimately, the utility, the adaptive value of any sensory system, is its capacity to gain information about the environment, information that an organism can act upon to increase its chances of surviving. For example, a creature that can detect light can perhaps position itself more favorably in relation to it. And a creature that can differentiate between the presence and absence of light can perhaps detect the looming shadow of an approaching predator and avoid the fate of its less-aware cousins. In this way, even a simple sea-dwelling creature could extract information from an array of light and act upon its meaning. (And we should note that arriving at this "meaning" and taking appropriate action is no intellectual feat, no act of inference; it is a response of a simple organism to a pattern of light and dark in its world.)

There is no master plan; change occurs in individuals by chance, and each change either helps a particular individual survive in its environment in its time or it does not. Yet, by such a process, we humans have acquired a complex and well-integrated perceptual system. To be sure, it is not a system that a good engineer might have designed from scratch. With hindsight, the human perceptual system (with its layering-on of structures, its duplication of parts, its complex interconnections) seems cobbled together. It is nonetheless amazingly efficient. But to say that it is efficient is to imply that it is efficient at doing something. What task is it that this system performs so efficiently? It is the extraction from the environment of information that is accurate enough to act upon. If the human perceptual system is in any sense "designed" this is what it is designed to do.

The Visual System

When we look at a video or movie screen, light (emitted or reflected) from the screen passes through the variable iris in the front of each of our eye spheres and is focused by a variable lens upon a tiny spot, the fovea, in the back of each eye. The fovea is part of the retina, which is composed of thin layers of specialized cells lying along the rear inner wall of the eye sphere.

There are several distinguishable layers of the retina, but for simplicity they can be described functionally in three groups: receptor cells, bipolar cells, and ganglion cells. The receptor cells, rods and cones, are sensitive to light and initiate electrical signals in response to the light patterns from external stimuli. These electrical signals pass by way of synapse to bipolar cells that coordinate the firings of the receptor cells (for example, by inhibiting receptors adjacent to a receptor that is firing, resulting in the heightening of visual contrast). The signals next pass by synapse to ganglion cells, which might be described as collector cells because they may collect the output of a number of receptor cells.

The peripheral area of the retina contains rods and a few cones, while the central fovea is composed mostly of cones. (Rods are not color sensitive, but cones are.) In the peripheral areas of the retina a single ganglion cell may serve as a collector for a number of receptor cells, while at the fovea there is practically a one-to-one correspondence between receptor cells and ganglion cells.[13] The signals from the ganglion cells are fed into the optic nerve fibers that exit from the eye through a passage in the rear of each sphere, a little to the nasal side of center. (At the place where the nerve leaves the eye, there is a blind spot on the retina.)

The optic nerve passes back from each eye, underneath the frontal lobes of the brain, to a point where the fibers meet. At their meeting place, called the optic chiasm, the fibers that have come from the nasal side of each retina, approximately half of all the fibers, cross over to the other side of the head. There they join the fibers that have remained, those which came originally from the temporal side of each retina, and this combination of fibers proceeds to the lateral geniculate body on either side of the central brain stem. The lateral geniculate is composed of layers of cells, and the fibers are fed into the layers in such a way as to keep separate the inputs from each eye. From the lateral geniculate, nerve fibers fan out to the visual cortex, the inner surfaces of the occipital lobes of the brain. At the visual cortex, the fibers synapse with the cells of the brain, creating a response field on each side representing half the visual field of the eyes. The cells in the visual cortex, arranged in rows and columns, communicate via a complex array of connections and fire in response to objects and events in the visual field.[14]

This is the present visual system that had its beginning millions of years ago when sea creatures developed light sensitive pits on the surface of their bodies and began to interact with the world on the basis of the new information available to them. This is the system whose architecture allows for processing in functional stages and at the same time maintains modularity (that is, processing may occur simultaneously in separate pathways but remains in sequence within a pathway, and information is kept segregated through as many stages of processing as is practical). This is the visual system that looks both at the natural world and at motion pictures.

The Auditory System

Through the senses we are able to gain information about the environment in which we live, with each sensory system tuned to a different spectrum of physical reality. Sight allows us to know where objects are located in the world, or more precisely, how we are situated among other objects, but if we sit in a darkened room, we learn nothing about the location of its objects. Conversely, we can hear in the dark, though our sense of hearing tells us almost nothing about the placement of objects—unless they move. If the cat jumps upon the piano or a book falls from a table we know instantly; our sense of hearing informs us of the event. Vision tells us where things are in space; hearing tells us when they move. And when they move, we are able to locate them in space.

Hearing is a complex interaction of ears, auditory nerves, and brain, much like seeing involves the eyes, optic nerves, and brain. The ear consists of outer, middle, and inner structures. The part of our ear that we usually refer to as an ear is called the pinna by anatomists and leads into the ear canal. The canal funnels incoming vibrations to the eardrum, which moves in response to the vibrating air column in the canal and transfers the pattern of vibration by means of three small bones, the mallus, the incus, and the stapes (hammer, anvil, and stirrup), to the membrane covering the opening to the cochlea, or inner ear.

The cochlea has the shape of an elongated sea shell tapering from a large end to a small end. A membrane called the basilar membrane is stretched the length of the cochlea and responds along its length to the different frequencies resonating at that position in the tapered cochlea. Upon the basilar membrane rest thousands of so-called hair cells. These hair cells fire in specific response to activity in different regions of the basilar membrane thus differentiating frequency as well as amplitude and timing (that is, the position denotes the frequency, the number of cells involved determines the amplitude or volume, and the onset indicates the timing).

The two ears, situated 180 degrees apart but cocked slightly forward, work together to help us locate sounds in space. The slight disparity in the timing of sounds reaching either ear allows for the computation of the locations of the events causing the sounds.

In addition to locating a sound's source in three-dimensional space, a major capacity of the auditory system is its ability to sort out the many competing sounds in the environment. We are, in fact, surrounded by a great variety of sounds coming from all directions, yet somehow the auditory system manages to isolate certain sounds from all the others, identify them, and place them correctly in space and time.

The visual and auditory systems are directly interfaced with a motion picture. When viewing a film, we are seeing, hearing, remembering, anticipating, forming concepts, and having emotional reactions—doing all those things the human mind is capable of doing. And we developed the capacity for all those things through the process of evolution. If we are to consider the relationship between ourselves and motion pictures, we must understand that it is at base ancient biology interfacing with recent technology.

Illusion and Computation

Motion pictures are not somehow exempt from ecological constraints because they are cultural artifacts rather than natural phenomena. As Gibson expressed so eloquently:

> Culture evolved out of natural opportunities. The
> cultural environment, however, is often divided into
> two parts, "material" culture and "non-material" cul-
> ture. This is a seriously misleading distinction, for
> it seems to imply that language, tradition, art, music,
> law, and religion are immaterial, insubstantial, or in-
> tangible whereas tools, shelters, clothing, vehicles,
> and books are not. . . . But let us be clear about this.
> . . . No symbol exists except as it is realized in sound,
> projected in light, mechanical contact, or the like. All
> knowledge rests on sensitivity.[15]

Let us consider the sense of vision to which motion pictures are in fact addressed. Perceptual psychologists for many years understood that light reflected from objects enters the eye through the pupil and is focused by the lens upon the retina and that the retina generates chemical and electrical signals that travel along the optic nerve to the lateral geniculate and then to the brain. What they did not understand very well, at least not until J. J. Gibson explained it, is what constitutes *visual information.*

Gibson proposed that information resides in the ambient array of light reflected from objects in the world. What is out there for the viewer to see are patterns of light that are continually shifting as the viewer moves through the environment. As the patterns change, some things vary and some stay the same. Things that do not vary, as the light changes and the viewer changes his point of view, constitute "invariants" in Gibson's terminology and define objects in the world. We learn where one object ends and another begins by walking around and looking at it or by observing the object (or individual) as it moves. Invariant patterns of light specify the object. Similarly, patterns observed during movement (of parts of the array or of oneself) provide information about the relationships of those objects. If an object, for instance, is in front of another object, one will be systematically covered or occluded and the other conversely uncovered as movement progresses. Information, then, consists of patterns of actual relationships between objects in the world. It is not something added, deduced, or inferred from raw data. The information contained in patterns of light is encountered directly by the visual system and processed immediately and continuously without the necessity of logical constructions such as deduction or inference. (This is what J. J. Gibson meant by *direct perception.*)

But what about illusions? Illusions are by definition nonveridical. How is it possible for humans, who like other animals are constructed to perceive information veridically, to succumb to illusion in general and to the illusions of motion pictures in particular? Gibson was not much interested in illusions. He could not understand why other psychologists spent so much time studying them. He rightly observed that they played no part in evolution and that in the natural world illusions were inconsequential. Motion pictures were not part of our environment as we developed our capacities for perception. Evolution could not have anticipated an environment cluttered with disembodied images and sounds. But nature's oversight does not make Gibson's ecological perspective irrelevant to understanding motion pictures. To the contrary, the ecological perspective, which allowed Gibson to gain insight into how an airplane pilot, while flying, perceives the world with a perceptual system designed by evolution for creatures who walk on the ground, allows us to take into account the problems of comprehending an environment cluttered with illusions, using a sensory system designed to perceive veridically the environment in which the system itself developed.

Here it is necessary to introduce the concept of computation even though Gibson did not like the idea. He insisted that perception is direct, and by that he meant that it does not require mediation or proceed by mental processes of the sort employed in logic such as deduction and inference. David Marr, neurophysiologist turned Artificial Intelligence (AI) theorist, offered a paradigm for visual processing consisting of three levels: first, a computational theory, a statement of what is being processed and why; next, an algorithm, a computational procedure; and finally, a hardware implementation, a physical implementation of the computation. Marr charged that Gibson "was misled by the apparent simplicity of the act of seeing."[16] Yet, even though he felt that Gibson's notion of the directness of perception was oversimplified, he nevertheless admired Gibson's theoretical insight.

Although algorithms and mechanisms are empirically more accessible, it is the top level, the level of computational theory which is critically important . . . the nature of computations that underlie perception depends more upon the computational problems that have to be solved than upon the particular hardware in which these solutions are implemented. . . . In perception, perhaps the nearest anyone came to the level of computational theory was Gibson (1966).[17]

Computational theory has developed considerably since Gibson's death in 1979 and Marr's death in 1982, and rather than contradicting the theory that Gibson developed and Marr accepted, contemporary computational theory offers mechanisms for its actuation. Cognitive psychologists Humphreys and Bruce in a recent book on visual cognition conclude that "it does seem possible to combine Gibsonian insights with a computational perspective . . . in which we ask not just what information is detected . . . but how it is detected."[18] For Humphreys and Bruce, Gibson provides the theoretical overview and Marr an approach to the computational means for its validation. The convergence of Gibson's ecological theory of perception with a computational analysis of processing provides the opportunity to build a new theoretical understanding of the motion picture. As we shall see, it is the fact that the perceptual systems go through the same computational procedures whether confronted with the real world or with synthesized shadows and sounds that allows for the existence of cinema.

At the risk of offending both Gibson and Marr, let us now focus our attention at the level of "hardware" for a moment and then work our way back to the level of theory. It turns out that the key to understanding illusion lies in the constraints of "hardware": in the limitations of the basic unit of neural processing—the neuron. There are different forms of specialized cells in the nerves and brain, but in general a nerve cell or neuron consists of an elongated cell body with extensions on both ends: an arboration of dendrites that carry signals to the cell body, and an axon that carries an electrical signal that is the output of the cell. The cell collects signals from other cells until its firing threshold is reached. It then suddenly depolarizes (allows an ion exchange through its walls) and sends an electrical signal down its axon.

Cells connect with each other at synapses, which the electrical signal does not transverse; instead, a chemical release is initiated that flows across the synapse and either excites or inhibits the next cell. The neuron, as the basic processor of the neural system, is relatively simple and dependable, but since a signal must be transformed from electrical to chemical form and back at every synapse, transmission proceeds relatively slowly.

This is the same phenomenon that Helmholtz had observed, but he concluded that time was necessary for the brain to carry out the process of unconscious inference; he, of course, had no notion of computational systems. We, on the other hand, do have models of such systems today and tend to do what others have done before us—that is, to use the latest technology as a model for explaining how the human mind works. It is possible to argue that such a practice is justified on the grounds that we have few other alternatives and that as technologies gain greater complexity they do indeed more closely approximate the complexity of the mind itself. Many contemporary researchers share Gibson's distaste for a concept of inference in connection with perception. For them, perceptions are not so much inferred as computed. But again, there is no little green man in one's brain doing mathematics. Computation occurs not in the sense of making logical mathematical constructions of the world but in the sense of cells being excited or inhibited, reaching threshold or not reaching threshold, firing or not firing.

If one views the neural system as a computational system which operates dependably but slowly (because of the transformation required from electrical to chemical form and back at every synapse), it is reasonable to speculate that strategies that speed up the system would have been very adaptive. Computational strategies or "shortcuts" that would minimize the time required to process visual information would have been retained. For example, it could be useful to be able to quickly detect the charge of a predator or the position of prey. If shortcuts became part of the hard-wired program and they worked in practically every situation encountered in the natural world, then they would have been selected by evolution and passed on, and we today would be the recipients of such a legacy. Evidence that this is indeed the case is provided by illusions. Illusions are experienced in those instances when the built-in shortcuts lead to nonveridical perceptions.

Vilayanur Ramachandran and Stuart Anstis proposed that at a fundamental level the visual system makes "assumptions" about the physical world in order to facilitate processing. They identified three such assumptions from a series of experiments on apparent motion: 1) that objects tend to remain in continuous existence, and if in motion tend to move along a straight path; 2) that objects are rigid, that is, all their parts tend to move together; and 3) that a moving object will progressively cover and uncover portions of the background.[19]

Ramachandran and Anstis maintain that these shortcuts are taken by the visual system in order to make processing more efficient and that generally the assumptions made by the system are constant. For example, by the first rule, if one sees a leopard running across a field and it disappears behind a bush, one assumes at the most basic levels of visual processing that the leopard emerging from the other side of the bush is the same leopard. If one catches sight of a few spots on the leopard's coat leaping across a chasm, one assumes, by the rule of rigidity, that the other spots leapt also. And one assumes by the third rule, occlusion, that as the leopard walks, the grass through which he passes will continually disappear at the edges of his head and shoulders and continually reappear at the edges of his hind legs and tail. To test each rule the researchers devised situations to induce apparent motion such as dots displaced spatially and flashing sequentially on a screen.

They found that indeed the rules were followed in visual processing even if what was seen was not veridical and even if viewers knew that what they were seeing was not what was really happening. For example, two dots were placed on the screen one over the other in one frame, and then in the

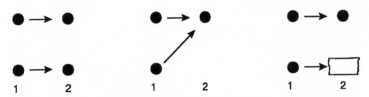

next frame the two dots were displaced slightly to the right. The result when shown in succession, as we would expect, was apparent motion—the dots seemed to move to the right. However, when the bottom dot in frame two was removed, the two dots from frame one were seen to converge on the remaining top dot in the second frame. That is, the bottom dot in frame one was seen to move in a diagonal path to the remaining dot at the top of frame two. More peculiarly, when a piece of tape was placed on the screen in the position of the bottom dot that had been removed, the two dots once again moved horizontally with the bottom dot seeming to "hide" behind the piece of tape. Clearly, the rules were being followed even though what was seen was nonveridical, that is, the bottom dot did not move at all. This is an illusion, one of those instances when the built-in shortcuts lead to nonveridical perceptions (see fig. 1).

In "hiding" the missing dot behind the piece of tape stuck to the screen, the visual system is doing more than merely filling in the missing dots between two points. It "assumes" that the dot "hid" from view behind the piece of tape rather than allow that the dot ceased to exist. Apparently in the presence of a plausible occluder, the continuity of existence rule operates to form a percept that is nonveridical (there is no second dot).

One might be tempted to conclude that the making of such

assumptions and the attribution of hiding to the behavior of a dot would require the involvement of higher level cognitive processes, but more likely, such processing is carried out at a low level in the visual system by neurons that programmatically excite and inhibit other neurons, not by the logic of language, but by the computational strategies built into the molecules of the system itself. Ramachandran and Anstis are specific on this point. Their experiments, they write, "were designed to eliminate the effects of high-level cognition; specifically, we flashed images at speeds too rapid to allow the brain to make thoughtful decisions about what it was seeing. Our results therefore suggest that low-level processes can, on their own, control the perception of apparent motion during the early stages of visual processing."[20]

Seeing the dot move behind the piece of tape and then move back to its original position is an illusion, one of those instances, rare in nature, when the visual system, following its internal program, creates a nonveridical perception, and thus reveals the program itself. This is at least a partial answer to the question of how it is possible for creatures such as ourselves, who were forged by evolution to obtain veridical information from our environment, to perceive illusions.

3
Capacities and Strategies

It may be difficult for film scholars steeped in the film theories of the past couple of decades to accept the idea that basic perceptual processing goes on without conscious direction or intellectual effort and that the strategies employed by our perceptual systems are not learned from our culture but are given to each of us by way of the genetic code we share as a member of a species. And if the idea that basic perceptual capacities were shaped by the forces of evolution is difficult to accept, then it may be even more difficult to accept the idea that higher-level capacities, including language and various aspects of cognition, are also built-in.

With regard to language, film theory suffers from the fact that film semioticians of the sixties and seventies chose to underpin their theories of film with the linguistics of Ferdinand de Saussure rather than that of Noam Chomsky. Saussure's approach cuts the signifier free from the signified and, in doing so, tends to emphasize the arbitrariness and conventionality of language. Saussure reasons that at a moment in time a word has a particular meaning for a speaker, a meaning determined by the speaker's experience in a language. And even if the word were to have an actual referent in the world, it is not that object in the world but an understanding of it that the speaker ultimately employs. That understanding, the signified, can change from moment to moment and therefore stands in no fixed relationship to the word, the signifier. And by extension, one can argue that much of the time we are talking not about objects, but about concepts for which no obvious referent exists in the world, concepts that are presumed to exist only in the consensus of culture. In such cases, the signifier again stands in no fixed relationship to the continually shifting culturally determined signified. Saussurian linguistics is the basis for the general argument that all that we know and all that constitutes our reality are the constructions of language and culture. And from this latter position it then follows: first, that what we know as reality has no physical or biological status, since all signifieds are constructions of their constitutive cultures, and second, that no concept, practice, or production can be privileged over any other.

Chomsky approaches language in a very different way. He offers among other things the concept of deep structures, that at a basic level all languages bear certain similarities because the underlying structure for language is innate. From such a perspective it is possible to reason that since only the human species has the capacity for language, since language is rather easily acquired by all members of the species across all cultures, and since all languages have basic features in common, then language must rest upon a biological basis. The capacities for language acquisition and language usage must have at some time in the past been encoded into our genetic makeup. Chomsky's approach is compatible with ecological theory and might have led, years ago, to an ecological film theory had the era of film semiotics embraced his linguistics rather than the linguistics of Saussure.

Capacities

Michael Gazzaniga in his recent book entitled *Nature's Mind* argues that "a group of species-specific devices, such as language systems, are now in place in us as a consequence of evolutionary events occurring thousands of years ago in the Pleistocene era."[1] Gazzaniga goes on to argue that we have specialized neural networks for all cognitive capacities, that we function by accessing the appropriate network for carrying out the task at hand, and that if we lack the circuitry for some task, then we simply cannot carry out that task, at least not in a direct way. "Our brains are built to process things in certain ways, and no amount of education or training can take us beyond these built-in characteristics. They have been selected out and have become, over millions of years, part of our repertoire of mental faculties."[2] Gazzaniga offers the phenomenon of creolization as an example. When groups of people speaking different languages are brought together, they develop, out of a necessity to communicate, a "pidgin" language with "crude syntax and no grammatical morphemes, embedding, or other trappings of a real language." Yet the children of such people do not grow up speaking the "pidgin" of their parents. "In a single generation they create a full-fledged language, a creole with auxiliaries, tense, and embedding. Clearly pidgins are unlearnable languages."[3]

Gazzaniga offers yet another example of the boundaries of species-specific capacities in the ability of human children to make certain attributions and the lack of it in chimpanzees. "By age six, children can, by interpreting facial expressions, distinguish between people who really know the answer to a problem as opposed to those who are guessing. Chimps with months of training never learn the art of attribution. Yet no child needs to attend school to be formally trained for it, for, as with speech and the analysis of the world into causal relations, social attribution comes naturally."[4]

Gazzaniga goes to great lengths to illustrate that the human brain is not a general purpose computing device simply engaging a gaggle of undifferentiated cells in pursuit of any task with which it is presented, but is instead a conglomerate of highly specialized neural circuits piled one upon another according to the contingencies of the environment during millions of years of evolution. Although these circuits are interconnected in very complex ways, they are nevertheless discrete modules with discrete and bounded capacities. And not only basic low level capacities, such as detecting motion or computing the direction from which a sound has come, but also higher level capacities, such as language and social attributions, are built-in.

Of course, Gazzaniga allows for the plasticity we know to exist in human intelligence. But he turns our notion of learning around. The traditional view is that we are born with certain potentials, but that we develop and refine our capacities as we learn from our environment. For Gazzaniga the environment does not instruct the individual, but instead selects from a multitude of already existing capacities. Evolution has given us the capacities appropriate to our species, more than we will ever use as individuals. Our environment "selects" the capacities that will be activated by confronting us with specific problems.

Gazzaniga has identified the general problem of accommodating the environment as consisting of selection versus instruction. Similarly, in the area of perception the controversy over the interaction with the environment has come down to selection versus construction. It is interesting that the idea of selection appears in both controversies, with the environment doing the selecting in the former, and the individual carrying out the selection in the latter. Selection as a mechanism carries a certain weight regardless of who the ostensible selector is, for it is compatible with what we know of the rest of biology. In both cases the mechanism of selection is offered by its advocates as an alternative to the more traditional instruction and construction models. The concept of selection is interesting to film theorists because it could apply to the way a filmmaker engages a spectator, and the way a spectator makes choices among the many patterns available from the screen.

E. H. Gombrich in *Art and Illusion* waded into the construction/selection controversy when he posited a hypothesis-forming visual system, one that actively seeks meaning and constantly samples and tests the visual world.[5] He apparently concurred with Bruner and Postman, whom he quoted as asserting that "all cognitive processes, whether they take the form of perceiving, thinking or recalling, represent 'hypotheses' which the organism sets up . . . They require 'answers' in the form of some further experience, answers that will either confirm or disprove them."[6]

Statements such as this may have led some to conclude that by hypothesis formation and testing in the perceptual act

Gombrich was talking about an organism that proceeds in its environment by constructing perceptions based upon partial or fragmentary evidence. Any misunderstandings were only deepened by statements such as the following: "It is the business of the living organism to organize, for where there is life there is not only hope, as the proverb says, but also fears, guesses, expectations which sort and model the incoming messages, testing and transforming and testing again."[7]

Some of his critics concluded that he was saying first, that a process of inference is required even at the most basic level of perception, and second, that one's perception of the world in general and art objects in particular are totally relative to one's fears, guesses, and expectations. By such statements he was thought to have offered support for a relativistic view of perception in general and of art in particular.[8] In his later writings he has attempted to rectify the situation and has asserted that he meant neither.[9] I am inclined to take him at his word.

Gibson, who was a friend of Gombrich, set out to clarify the use of such terms as *hypothesis formation* and *expectation* with regard to the perceptual act. In reference to the usual laboratory setup in which a rat learns to run a maze, push a lever, and receive food, Gibson cautioned: "To call the process one of predicting an event and then verifying its occurrence makes it seem an intellectual accomplishment and dignifies the rat undeservedly. The rat's perception is more primitive than this."[10] For Gibson and perhaps for Gombrich, too, hypothesis formation and testing is a metaphorical description of a very low-level, primitive process in visual perception and not a description of a high-level cognitive inference performed on the part of the perceiver.

In delineating his theory of ecological optics, Gibson avoided some of the pitfalls that may have bedeviled Gombrich, but in doing so he created a storm of controversy that still rages. He held that we do not stumble around collecting random information and risking overload, but instead, we

move around our world purposefully seeking the things we
need in order to live our lives. Gibson called these things
affordances, and he held that in our very perception of an object
or event is embedded its affordance for us. (If it holds no
affordance for us, we may ignore it altogether.)

The concept of affordance is one of the most difficult to
grasp of Gibson's insights into how we interact with our environment, yet this concept, or one serving the same purpose,
is essential to a theory that would begin to explain how one
interacts meaningfully with the world. His theory rests upon
the assumption that we do not, as some have suggested, arrive
at meaning by enhancing impoverished stimuli emanating
from the world (or from a motion picture). The world is overdetermined rather than underdetermined; there are many different sets of information, many different affordances, for any
given object or event. We need only pick up one of the many
meaningful patterns of information available to us. Which
of them we see is much influenced by learning and experience.

Ulric Neisser illustrated this point brilliantly using the example of a chessboard. The chess master, he writes,

> quite literally sees the position differently—more
> adequately and comprehensively—than a novice or
> a non-player would. Of course, even the non-player
> sees a great deal: the chessmen are of carved ivory,
> the knight resembles a horse, the pieces are (perhaps)
> arrayed with a certain geometric regularity. A young
> child would see still less: that the pieces would fit
> into his mouth, perhaps, or could be knocked over.
> A newborn infant might just see that "something"
> was in front of him. To be sure, he is not mistaken
> in this: something is in front of him. The differences
> among the perceivers are not matters of truth and
> error but of noticing more rather than less.[11]

Perception, then, is a matter of selection. One does not take
in any and all available stimulation and filter out those un-

wanted or unused. Only some of the information is selected, and what learning enables one to do is to notice more, to become a more skillful perceiver of events and affordances.

An affordance is a relationship, or potential relationship, between us and our environment, and a relationship can be enhanced or changed by learning. But while there may be many possible affordances for an object, the list is not infinite. (Perhaps it is the implicit testing of the limit of the concept of affordance that makes an act like Marcel Duchamp's declaration of a urinal as "art" so titillating, for outside the category of "art object," the list of possible affordances of a urinal is fairly short.) Constraints are placed upon the relationship by both the perceiver and the world. Again, to quote Neisser: "No choice is ever free of the information on which it is based. Nevertheless, that information is selected by the chooser himself. On the other hand, no choice is determined by the environment directly. Still, that environment supplies the information that the chooser will use."[12]

Both Gibson and Gombrich regarded the viewer as participating in just such a dynamic relationship with his world. They both considered the selection of useful perceptual information as the primary goal of the active viewer. Perhaps it is Gombrich's terminology that is misleading, for his emphasis on hypothesis formation and testing (translating nicely into his description of the schema and correction, making and matching processes in the development of painting) is no more or less than his conviction that the human organism is not a passive but an active one, an organism that displays what F. C. Bartlett called the "effort after meaning," which Gombrich reminds us begins the moment we open our eyes.

That meaning-seeking nature of the human mind is the fundamental assumption shared by Gombrich and Gibson, and it is this assumption that allowed Ulric Neisser to formulate a theory of perception and cognition which incorporates the notion of hypothesizing and testing into what he calls a "perceptual cycle." In such a perceptual cycle, individuals interact with information from the world in a process of schema and exploration. Exploration of the environment is guided by the schema, which is in turn modified by the perceptual experience such that the next perception of a similar object and event will be directed by a different schema. Therefore, a person's next perception of the same object or situation will perhaps be extended or elaborated. Neisser writes: "In my view, the cognitive structures crucial for vision are the anticipatory schemata that prepare the perceiver to accept certain kinds of information rather than others and thus control the activity of looking. Because we can see only what we know how to look for, it is these schemata (together with the information actually available) that determine what will be perceived."[13]

It is important to realize that this is very different from saying that we see only what we expect to see or that we see only what we know. The process of vision and cognition for Neisser is a process that is selective rather than constructive. As Neisser puts it: "Perceptual schemata disambiguate by selecting a particular alternative, not by adding more evidence for it."[14] The particular schemata (expectations) with which viewers approach the environment prepare them to pick up one set of information rather than another. The viewers' schemata will determine which of those is salient, which of them will be perceived. Thus the capacity to "see" a given configuration on a chess board illustrates both the role of learning in informing affordances and the role of affordances in the act of perception.

Resolution of Ambiguity

The potential for ambiguity is a hazard for a perceptual system that must achieve veridicality, not only because we may each see different affordances in a chess board, but also because our biological ancestors developed multiple sensory systems. Beyond the sensory organs themselves, our ancestors developed elaborate systems for utilizing each sense for extracting useful information from the environment. J. J. Gibson put it this way: "Each eye is positioned in a head that is in turn positioned on a trunk that is positioned on legs that maintain the posture of the trunk, head and eyes relative to the surface of support. Vision is a whole perceptual system, not a channel of sense. One sees the environment not with the eyes, but with the eyes-in-the-head-on-the-body-resting-on-the-ground."[15]

Survival demanded more than merely seeing, hearing, and smelling. It demanded looking, listening, and sniffing. The processes of evolution forged a purposive, information-gathering, meaning-seeking animal driven to make sense of its world. What one must realize is that as meaning-seeking creatures we are not outside the environmental system looking in at it. We are inside the system, part of it, affecting and being affected by the environment. Ours is an ecological relationship, an ongoing, dynamic interaction with the environment.

In such a context erroneous information is worthless, perhaps even dangerous, for the value of the information is in its capacity to inform action. To that end, our perception developed well beyond the passive registration of incoming data; it became an overtly active process with a winner-takes-all strategy for settling conflicts. It remains so today.

Let me offer an example of the winner-takes-all strategy at the initial stages of visual perception. When one views the simplest of conflicting stimuli—two slides consisting of sets of lines tilted at an angle of forty-five degrees presented stereoscopically so that what is presented is a set of lines leaning to the left in one eye and a similar set of lines leaning to the right in the other eye—what one may see first is a grid composed of both sets of lines. But very quickly the lines in one eye will disappear, leaving only the set of lines in the other eye (see fig. 2). The patterns may alternate, that is, one may first see the lines available to one eye and then those available to the other, but one cannot hold both sets of lines in perception simultaneously.[16] This is a classic instance of binocular rivalry and is well known to students of perception. I suggest that it may serve as the limiting case for all perception.

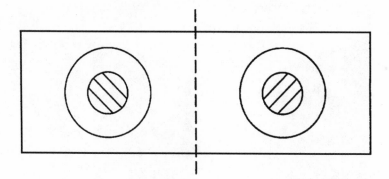

Fig. 2. Viewed stereoptically, these two stimuli produce the perception of a cross-hatched pattern that quickly gives way to alternating perceptions of first one set of lines and then the other. Place a card upon the dotted line in such a way that each eye sees only one bull's-eye in order to produce the effect.

The perceptual system cannot tolerate ambiguity; it must obtain information it can act upon. Indecision is potentially fatal. The system does not mush things together into a pseudo-reality: it makes choices, even if each choice asserts itself intermittently. Binocular rivalry is an instance of alternating percepts at very early stages in the visual process, but there are many more such phenomena that occur at later stages in perception. There are, for example, a number of so-called ambiguous forms that are well known to students of perception: the vase/face, the necker cube, the Escher staircase, among others. In these instances, as in binocular rivalry, the visual system is presented with two incompatible sets of information. In the same figure one cannot, for example, see faces and a vase at the same time, though the information for each of those percepts is contained within the ambiguous figure. The viewer consequently alternates between seeing faces and then a vase and then faces again (see fig. 3).

These figures illustrate the winner-takes-all strategy of the human perceptual system. If the system were designed so that some slippage occurred between reality and perception, or if

Fig. 3. Face/vase figure first introduced by Danish
psychologist John Edgar Rubin in 1915.

conflicting information were averaged or compromised, then
every act would be based upon inaccurate information. This
would not be an effective strategy for survival. The odds are
far better if the system picks one set of information to act
upon.

The strategy of winner-takes-all may be built into the structure of the brain at all levels—perhaps in a way that is described by chaos theory. A chaotic system is so poised that
small inputs can result in massive synchronized outputs. In
the brain there may be an underlying order that allows large
numbers of neurons to switch abruptly from one task to another.[17] The metaphor of crystallization is sometimes used to
describe such a system; its action appears to be one of dynamic
flux which suddenly crystalizes into a coherent form. It has
been suggested that the mechanism of such crystallization is

synchrony, that is, groups of cells suddenly achieving synchrony with each other and firing simultaneously.[18]

We should note that cells in the brain are always in an active state, firing several times a second even while at rest. The neural system exists in this poised, alert state, and when cells are stimulated, as through sensory input, they fire more rapidly. But it turns out that stimulated cells not only increase their firing rates; they may also stimulate other cells to fire in synchrony with them in what might be called a pattern of activation.

It is interesting to note that in the ongoing enterprise of cognitive modeling in artificial intelligence (comprising a significant part of current cognitive science), many researchers have chosen to employ a winner-takes-all strategy in their attempts to simulate the functioning of the human cognitive system. It is just such a strategy that I would suggest is at the heart of an understanding of the film viewing experience.

A motion picture contains two sets of information: one for a three-dimensional world and one for a flat screen. As J. J. Gibson might say, it is both a scene and a surface. I would suggest that at the most basic perceptual level the film viewer alternates between the two percepts frequently and without significant distraction from the events unfolding in the three-dimensional world of the alternate percept. This continuous push-pull at a perceptual level may well form the basis of the dual awareness of scene and surface that is the experience of the motion picture.

The moviegoer's response is consistent with the resulting awareness of real-but-not-real that accompanies film viewing. Even in the most engrossing of movies, the dual nature of the film viewing experience serves to prevent moviegoers from acting upon the information obtained from the screen (we do not get up and run out of the theater at the appearance of the monster) and at the same time allows us to remain involved in the events taking place on the screen.

But it is possible for the perceptual alternation we experience to become obtrusive, if only momentarily. For example, we may find ourselves among colossal sandstone simulations of bundled papyrus reeds along with James Bond and the character we identify as "Jaws" playing out a dangerous game of hide and seek. Our eyes search the array of massive vertical columns for a glimpse of the lethal "Jaws." But our vision is blocked by one of the columns, and so we move our head and lean sideways, craning our neck to see around it. In the real world, such an action would result in the phenomenon of motion parallax, which is to say that everything in our field of vision would move in relation to our movement (as described in chap. 4), but in this instance nothing moves when we move, and our feedback system, which compensates for our own movements, is thwarted. Suddenly the picture flattens, the edges of the screen intrude, and we are once again sitting in a theater watching a grainy colored shadow on a beaded screen.

This is the experience of film viewing; there is information in the visual array for both a three dimensional fictional world and for a flat screen with shadows playing upon it. But these are incompatible perceptions; we must choose one and only one of them, and we do—alternately. It is not a matter of being in a semihypnotic state in a darkened theater. It is not a matter of suspending disbelief. It is not a matter of being "positioned" as a spectator or "sutured" into a text, and it has nothing to do with dreaming. It is instead our perceptual system alternating between two incompatible sets of information.

But we should note that the competition is not equal, the sides are unbalanced. In a purely informational sense the three dimensional array contains more information than the two dimensional one. Motion, as Gibson has taken some pains to point out, is a most significant part of the process of perception, and there is more motion in the three-dimensional array of a motion picture than in the two-dimensional one. A constant change of scene occurs through both editing and camera movement, which provides not only motion parallax but also a dynamic and complex optical flow to the perceiver. The successive changes in position (of the camera and therefore the spectator) orient the spectator to the events taking place on the screen. Moreover, as social animals, we spectators are sensitive to the events of the narrative; the information being provided by the actions of the characters in the three-dimensional array is of more consequence to us than the information provided by either the colored shadows moving across a flat screen or the spectator sitting next to us eating his popcorn. We are meaning-seeking creatures, and the meanings in a film viewing situation are to be found in the diegetic world of the motion picture.

Categorization

In the discussion so far, I have gone to some lengths to demonstrate two important characteristics of human perception first made explicit by Gibson: 1) that inferential and intellectual processes are not required for perception, even in its most complex possibilities; and 2) that the recognition of affordances of objects and events in an environment are inherent in the act of perception. To paraphrase Gibson, a fish can perceive the affordance of a ledge to hide under, and so can we. Such perception cannot be a high-level intellectual activity. If these two related insights are important to the study of perception, they are a priceless gift to film theory, for they open the door to our understanding of how we experience a motion picture.

Central nervous systems of both fish and humans are modular. They could not be otherwise, for neither were conceived full blown, but were built by a process of layering on new modules over old. Humans simply possess a couple of newer modules that fish lack. And one of the most blindly arrogant mistakes we could make would be to assume that since we have acquired the new cerebral cortex module, the neocortex, we no longer use the older modules, or that because a particular process occurs at a lower level in the system that it is less important than a "higher-level" process. To the contrary, the "lower-level" process is phylogenetically older, more basic and more compelling. There is good evidence that not only do we continue to use the old modules, but that when conflicts of processing arise between modules the old usually overrides the new.[19]

The anatomic modules of the central nervous system are interconnected into functional modules which are further interconnected with other parts of the system. To use a computer analogy, the arrangement seems to be less like a central mainframe with workstations than a room full of PCs all interconnected with each other. While most living creatures get along fine without an enlarged neocortex such as humans possess, it apparently is the site of a cornucopia of capacities, such as language, mathematics, abstraction, symbolization, willful learning, internally generated thought, and the ability to focus attention at will.

Through his insight that perception is phylogenetically old and basic and that affordances are an integral part of perception itself, Gibson gave us no less than a way of grasping the relationship between perceiving and thinking. Perceiving an affordance is a basic form of categorization. And as Ulric Neisser has demonstrated, categorization is an activity that has an intellectual as well as an ecological basis. Drawing upon the work of Eleanor Rosch, he posits three illustrative levels of categorization: a basic level, a superordinate level, and a subordinate level. For example, a chair might belong in a basic level category, with furniture and rocking chair in superordinate and subordinate categories respectively. Categorization begins with the basic level categories, categories defined by appearance and function. Items in the basic level categories tend to look alike, and our interaction with them tends to be similar.[20]

Gibson's concepts of invariants (aspects of the visual array that persist through changes in illumination and point of view) and affordances (relationships between an organism and its environment) apply directly to the process of basic level categorization, where objects are categorized according to their affordances on the basis of appearance. For example, one might while walking see in the trunk of a fallen tree the affordance of sitting. The perception of such an affordance does not require language, and it is not a matter of naming; one has simply perceived a place to sit, which we may for the purpose of discussion call a "seat." It is a seat because it looks like a place one could sit, that is, by appearance and affordance. One could bring a portion of the tree home and use it to sit upon; at this point one might name it, perhaps calling it a chair. It is perhaps an intellectual leap to link a chair to other items such as tables, beds, and chests of drawers into a superordinate category. Such a leap might require inference and a level of abstraction available only to humans. And of course assigning a name to such a category requires language.

It is, then, from the basic, ecologically driven act of perception and categorization that we proceed, by way of inference, deduction, abstraction, and so forth to other levels of categorization—the superordinate or subordinate categories. Such hierarchies, according to Neisser, "often have more than three levels . . . but there is always at least one basic level near the middle."[21] This basic level category is central to our perception of motion pictures, where it is, after all, the appearances of objects and events that are recorded by the camera. As Neisser recognizes: "These principles apply even to the perception of television images and movies and (recently) holograms, where optical structure is made to appear without any real environmental substrate. No objects are actually present in such displays, but in a sense perception is still direct."[22]

In viewing a movie, we bring everything we know to the experience—what we know about other movies and movie conventions, our cultural knowledge, our specific background and education. We make inferences; we put things together and draw conclusions; we go through all of the higher level mental activities we as humans are capable of. But all of this we might do in a *discussion* of film.

What makes the *viewing* of a film different is the surrogate visual array on the screen, which makes possible the perceptual basis upon which all knowledge rests. This perceptual basis is the common denominator, shared even cross-culturally. The objects and events and affordances for film characters can be perceived at the basic level. (In an action adventure film, for example, there may be little more than this to the movie at all. But the very fact that such films function at this level makes them universally accessible.)

Movies can and do go beyond basic level categorization. They can draw upon the viewer's knowledge of movie conventions, cultural assumptions, and so forth. Yet it is the perceptual basis of the film viewing experience that allows these intellectual and cultural abstractions to be incorporated into both understanding and emotion. It is the perceptual basis of the filmic experience that gives a movie a palpable sense of reality.

Summary

Perceptions are probably not constructed; motion pictures most certainly are. Every element is scripted, designed, and choreographed; little is left to chance. In the Hollywood system, the responsibility for constructing a motion picture may be said to fall upon the director. He must pass judgment upon what the writer writes, what the actor performs, and what the cinematographer photographs. More than that, he is responsible for the construction of the fictional world of the film and the giving of laws by which it is governed. He goes about his job by alternating between two very different roles, creator and viewer. It is a process described by Gombrich as making and matching. As creator, he constructs (makes) a bit of the movie as he contrives to make the fictional real, and then as viewer he tests its plausibility, testing to see if the response it evokes in him "matches" the response he wants to elicit from his viewers. By this process he constructs the film to convey particular meanings; he makes selections for the viewer. Within the fictional world he chooses affordances for the characters, he narrows their options and ours. In the end, the affordances are generally preselected, the meanings implicit, and if he has done his work well the fiction is compelling, the actions and events take on a "reality" and are totally plausible within the frame of the world created. But we, the viewers, are usually unaware of the narrowness of the options. If the director has done his job well, we are caught up in a seamless world where events unfold causally toward seemingly inevitable conclusions. The movie is not ours to "read." It is ours to experience as we interact with its complex program. After the fact we are, of course, free to reflect upon and interpret the experience in any way we like. But it is only to the extent that a director understands (by alternating roles as viewer and creator) how we will interact that he can construct a motion picture. It is only to the extent that he can construct a motion picture which is compatible with the way we perceive the world that we experience his experience at all. It is a testament to the universality of human perception that he *can* and we *do*.

4

Some Problems Reconsidered

Having laid some groundwork in ecological perception, perhaps I can now address a few of the problems that have over the years captured the attention of film scholars but resisted coherent explication. 1) How is it possible for a succession of still frames to create a compelling illusion of smooth, continuous motion? 2) What is the nature of depth in the motion picture? Is perspective a convention of culture? 3) The presence of *color constancy* in natural vision regardless of color temperature, and the lack of such a constancy in photography, has aggravated cinematographers and baffled film scholars for half a century. How does color temperature really work?

Flicker and Motion Perception

The technical apparatus of the motion picture has remained essentially the same since the time of its invention at the end of the last century. Of course the projector lies on its side now, and the film is held by gravity upon large platters rather, than upright reels. The film itself has undergone considerable advancement from black and white to color to much better color, and there is greater latitude in the amount of light required for proper exposure. The sound system has gone from early attempts at synchronous sound, to nonsynchronous live accompaniment to a synchronous sound and picture system, to digital recreations of live sound. (Clearly, the most striking advances in film technology have been in the areas of sound and special effects, both the result of great advances in electronics over the last two decades.) Yet for all the refinements in apparatus, a succession of frozen images are still projected upon a screen at the rate of twenty-four frames per second.[1]

The projection rate illustrates one of the many instances in which the motion picture apparatus was modified to accommodate the viewer's perceptual apparatus. Edison films of 1895 and 1896 were reportedly shot at approximately forty frames per second in order to minimize flicker.[2] Such a rate was impractical for several reasons, not the least of which were the expense and difficulty in obtaining and handling long pieces of film. A more economical rate was sought, and by trial and error it was discovered that images photographed at rates slower than sixteen frames per second resulted in the perception of excessively jerky motion and annoying flicker. Therefore, sixteen frames per second became the nominal standard, although since cameras were hand-cranked, frame rates depended precariously upon the camera operator's skill. The practice developed of cranking the camera at twelve to fifteen frames per second, then projecting at seventeen frames per second or faster.[3] The result was that motion picture characters moved about more quickly than normal, and considerable jerkiness and flicker remained. With the advent of sound it was discovered that at sixty feet per minute (sixteen frames per second) slight variations in speed produced annoying fluctuations in sound quality and high frequencies were impossible to produce. The outcome of further experimentation was that Western Electric set a speed of ninety feet per minute (twenty-four frames per second), and this became the industry standard.[4] Sound quality thus benefited from the greater speed of the soundtrack, and coincidentally, the picture projection rate moved to within acceptable limits for the human visual system. The standard rate for motion picture photography and projection in the United States was thus established on the basis of trial and error, coupled with convenience and economy, but with little knowledge of the mechanisms of visual perception. Yet it was the human perceptual system that set the limits to which the cinematic apparatus had to conform.

The projection rate of twenty-four frames per second led to the experience of smooth motion and adequate sound quality, but as with the rate of sixteen frames per second a perceptible flicker remained. (Motion and flicker are separable perceptual phenomena.) With both motion picture cameras and projectors (each being a kind of mirror twin of the other), the film proceeds intermittently.[5] That is to say, a motion picture is made up of a strip of still images which were made by exposing them one at a time as the film was stopped and held still for the duration of the exposure. When projected, the film must again be stopped and held still while the image is projected upon the screen. The film therefore proceeds intermittently through the projector, moving then stopping, then moving again, for each of the thousands of frames that make up a feature length motion picture. If the image were projected upon the screen while the film is in motion, the viewer would see only a blurred image. A rotating shutter is therefore placed in position to block out the light of the projector lamp while the film is moving.

The simplest version of such a shutter was a circular disc with one half opaque and the other half cut away. When the opaque half of the disc rotated in front of the beam of light, the next frame of film was advanced. When the cut away half of the disc approached the light beam, the film came to a complete stop and the still image was projected upon the screen, and so on for the entire film. The viewer saw twenty-four images and coincidentally twenty-four flashes of light each second, one flash each time a frame of picture was projected. (Between the flashed pictures was darkness.)

Anyone who has ever played with a strobe light knows, there is a discernible flicker at twenty-four flashes per second, and the disturbing flicker sensation disappears when the flicker rate is increased. The ingenious solution to the flicker problem in the motion picture was to create a multi-bladed shutter that would increase the flicker rate. With the film projector it was possible to take the circular disc that had been divided into two parts and divide it into four parts, with the sections alternately opaque and cut away, leaving two opaque blades. The flicker rate could thus be doubled. That is, the projector would still be projecting images at the rate of twenty-four per second, but each of those projected images would be interrupted in the middle with the extra blade of the shutter, the flicker rate thereby being increased to forty-eight cycles per second. Interrupting the image on the screen with a period of darkness was compensated for by using a brighter light source, and it greatly diminished the flickering. The next step was easy: if a two blade shutter created a flicker rate of forty-eight flashes per second, then a three blade shutter would create a flicker rate of seventy-two flashes per second. At the latter rate, the viewer was no longer able to detect the flicker, and the luminosity appeared consistent.

The point is that the motion picture apparatus was constructed and modified by trial and error until it interfaced successfully with the human visual (and auditory) system. We are now in a position to know *why* the interface was successful. With regard to the flicker, for example, careful research has established that the precise frequency at which flicker disappears depends upon the intensity of the light, its wavelength, its duration, the relative area of the visual field illuminated, the part of the retina stimulated, and the age of the viewer. Taking all these things into consideration, we can say that in the typical motion picture viewing situation, flicker fusion is experienced at about fifty flashes per second. When the developers of the film projector increased the flicker rate to seventy-two flashes per second they had gotten it well past the capacity of any individual viewer to discriminate between flashes. The result is attributable to a function of the neuronal networks of the visual system, which will be discussed, but first let us consider the mechanics of the video display.

The projection rate for television was established as a matter of convenience. The frequency of alternation of electricity can be set arbitrarily. Most countries in Europe generate electricity at fifty hertz, or fifty alternations in direction per second. In this country the standard is sixty hertz. In a video tube a stream of electrons, emitted from a cathode at the back of the tube and directed by electromagnets, systematically "writes" a picture upon a phosphorescent screen. (We view the resulting image from the other side of the screen.) The beam scans back and forth in straight horizontal lines as it "writes" the image. Where the electrons strike the screen it glows bright for an instant. Each "frame" of a video image is a still picture just like each frame of a motion picture. But when video engineers were faced with the problem of how many "frames" to present each second, twenty-four turned out to be an awkward number. Sixty was a much more convenient number, because the switching of "frames" could be linked to the sixty alternations per second of the current. But sixty images per second was incompatible with the twenty-four frames per second already established by the motion picture industry. The solution was to keep the sixty images per second but to "write" one half of each "frame," that is, every other line, at a time. But instead of scanning every frame of film twice, every other frame was scanned three times, thus converting twenty-four frames of film picture to thirty frames of video.[6] The result is that video in the United States presents thirty "frames" of still pictures each second and flickers at the rate of sixty times each second. Both rates are similar to those employed in the motion picture and are well above the minimum frequencies required by the human visual system. (This is a description of flicker fusion and not an explanation of motion in the motion picture.)

Most interesting for those who would understand motion pictures, research into motion perception has discovered that there are at least two categories of apparent motion. In research spanning more than two decades, Paul Kolers focused upon several ways in which the perception of apparent motion and of real motion differ. In 1971, he and J. R. Pomerantz tested the effect of spatial intermittency on the illusion of motion. They found that when two elements appeared on the screen, good illusory motion was seen with proper timing. (This is the usual binary or two-element display, the limiting case for apparent motion.) When four, eight, or sixteen elements appeared, smooth continuous motion was never attained. However, with thirty-two or sixty-four or more elements, smooth continuous motion was again perceived. Therefore, if smooth continuity of motion was rated as a function of number of elements presented, the result would be a U-shaped curve. Kolers concluded: "It seems there is no necessary continuity of processing between spatially separated and spatially contiguous flashes; the ways the visual system constructs the two perceptions of motion seems to be quite different."[7] This suggests that multi-element or closely spaced displays may be mediated by the same mechanisms as real motion, while more widely spaced displays (the usual two-flash displays used to demonstrate apparent motion) involve a different type of processing.

These two types of apparent motion, the perception of motion from multi-element or closely spaced displays and the perception of motion resulting from more widely spaced displays, have come to be termed *short-range* and *long-range* apparent motion respectively. The establishment of the defining characteristics of the two processes has been the focus of much of the research done in apparent motion in recent years.

Biederman-Thorson, Thorson, and Lange, for instance, presented subjects with two dots so closely spaced as to be perceived as a single dot when flashed simultaneously. When those same dots were flashed sequentially, motion was clearly perceived. Like Kolers, these experimenters concluded that perception of motion accompanying very small dot separation, that is, short-range apparent motion (which they term the *fine grain illusion*), may involve a different level of processing than apparent motion induced by more widely spaced stimuli. Moreover, they specifically suggested that the fine-grain illusion may share a common base with the perception of real motion.[8]

Oliver Braddick, working with random-dot patterns, arrived at a similar conclusion. He demonstrated that motion was perceived between two random-dot patterns only when the dots were displaced about a quarter of a degree of visual angle or less.[9] (This was the same spatial limit suggested by Kolers and Pomerantz for the perception of apparent motion with multi-element displays.)

Further support for the contention that short-range and long-range apparent motion may be mediated by different mechanisms comes from evidence that short-range apparent motion can generate motion aftereffects (for example, the waterfall or spiral illusion). Briefly, if one looks for a time at a pattern (such as a rotating spiral or flowing water) moving in a particular direction, and then looks at a stationary pattern, the stationary pattern will appear to move slowly in the opposite direction. The movement aftereffects are, of course, also produced by real movement, but there is a lack of existing evidence that such aftereffects can be generated by long-range apparent motion.[10]

Closely connected to the generation of movement aftereffects is the evidence that short-range apparent motion stimulates motion detectors at a very low level in the visual cortex. J. Timothy Petersik, reviewing research on the two-process distinction in apparent motion in 1989, concludes: "On the basis of the studies reviewed here, one may postulate that both short-range AM [apparent motion] and RM [real motion] are adequate stimuli for low-level neural motion detectors and that long-range AM provides only a weak stimulus for such detectors."[11] Once again, the evidence seems to indicate notable differences between short-range and long-range processes in apparent motion, while pointing to notable similarities between the characteristics of short-range apparent motion and the perception of real motion.

Clinical evidence also supports the distinction. It is now known that in the human visual system motion is processed separately from form and color.[12] A condition known as *akinetopsia* (resulting from a lesion in area V5 of the prestriate cortex) is characterized by the inability to see objects in motion. Such patients can neither see nor understand the world in motion; they have no trouble seeing objects at rest, but the objects disappear when placed in motion. Other patients suffer from a type of form imperception (often accompanied by achromatopsia: seeing the world only in shades of gray). These patients have great difficulty identifying forms when stationary but little or no difficulty in doing so when those forms are in motion.[13] For our purposes, the most interesting facet of the latter pathology is the penchant of such patients for watching television.[14] These patients who are "blind" to still images in the real world can nevertheless see the succession of still images presented on the television screen. Apparently the temporal and spatial parameters of the presentation of the television images are sufficient to engage the motion processing module of the brain.

For students of the motion picture, the psychophysical research, the clinical research, and the physiological research all lead to an understanding that not only is the traditional *persistence of vision* explanation of motion in the motion picture inadequate, but that explanations associated with apparent movement such as Wertheimer's *phi* movement are also inadequate and misleading. It is more likely that motion in the motion picture is a result of the indistinguishability of the small frame to frame changes in a movie from the continuous changes that occur in real motion in nature, resulting in the former being processed by the networks of the visual system as real motion.[15] The visual system simply fails to detect the real difference between the successive changes in the static frames of a motion picture and the continuous changes of natural motion. This is another occasion when visual processing, following the internal rules of the system, results in a percept that is nonveridical—it is an illusion.

Motion and Form

Considerable evidence exists from both psychophysical and neurophysiological studies for a distinction between motion and form processing. In several different studies employing psychophysical methods, S. M. Anstis has demonstrated that movement is mediated on a point-for-point basis by brightness rather than form and maintains that motion perception can precede pattern recognition. In a set of experiments using Bela Julesz's random-dot stereograms, Anstis found that the random-dot figures, which produced depth when viewed binocularly, were seen in motion when viewed in monocular alternation.[16] (In such a stereogram, the images are composed of random dots. There is no indication of form available to monocular vision. The form appears only when viewed binocularly.) This, too, could be interpreted as evidence that prior form processing need not precede motion perception, in the same way that Julesz has made the argument that form processing is not needed for the perception of depth in his random-dot stereograms.[17]

Neurophysiological findings have provided further evidence for the distinction between form and motion processing. In fact, Livingstone and Hubel have gone much further and have described a visual system that processes motion, form, and color separately. Working with Macaque monkeys, they were able to trace the anatomical and functional pathways of the visual system from the retina of the eye, through the lateral geniculate, and into the visual cortex of the brain. What they found is generally consistent with what had been learned about visual processing from psychophysical studies but quite astounding in terms of both anatomical layout and implications for processing strategies. The visual system is not designed the way one would design it if one were starting from scratch. But, of course, it was not designed from scratch. It developed through the indifferent evolutionary processes of diversity and natural selection, by adding onto what already existed. The primate visual system is as a house built by adding onto a smaller house, with materials that happened to be at hand, on the basis of whatever worked to keep out the cold. The resulting structure is, however, amazingly efficient.

Livingstone and Hubel found that there are two anatomically and functionally different processing systems for vision.

One they call the magno system, named for the group of large cells (magno) they found in the lateral geniculate, and the other the parvo system, in deference to the grouping of relatively smaller cells (parvo) also found in the lateral geniculate. The two systems maintain their separation from the eye to the lateral geniculate and through several levels of processing in the cortex, although they share information at certain levels of processing in the brain.

Livingstone and Hubel surmise that the magno system developed first phylogenetically, and that the parvo system developed later probably as the result of genetic duplication of the magno system. The newer parvo or small-celled system is ten times the magnitude of the magno system and performs functions not available to the magno system like the processing of color.

The older magno system performs functions that were no doubt crucial to the survival of our distant ancestors: the detection of motion, the separation of objects from their background, and the positioning of those objects in three-dimensional space. Light from objects in the world interacts with the magno system through the large ganglion (collector) cells in the retina. Color and the specifics of shape are ignored from the outset. But there are advantages; the system can operate at low light levels and at relatively high speed, and it can calculate where something is in space and in what direction it is moving, all the while compensating for its own head and eye movements. Indeed,

the magno system is capable of what seem to be the essential functions of vision for an animal that uses vision to navigate in its environment, catch prey, and avoid predators. The parvo system, which is well developed only in primates, seems to have added the ability to scrutinize in much more detail the shape, color, and surface properties of objects, creating the possibility of assigning multiple visual attributes to a single object and correlating its parts.[18]

From the beginning natural selection favored those creatures who reached out to the world around them. Those who
had little or no information about the outside world simply
stood to be grazed upon by their predators. Those who could
sense the approach of a predator could take evasive action.
Those who could locate other creatures precisely in space
and distinguish between them could become predators themselves. Therefore, the more information a creature could obtain the better. It should come as no surprise that primates,
like ourselves, are the inheritors of a visual system that
extracts an amazing amount of information from the small
bundle of light rays that enter the pupils of our eyes. At the
level of the retina, the rods respond to brightnesses and the
cones respond differentially to wavelengths of light (some to
yellow and red, some to green, and some to green and blue).
This information is sorted at the lateral geniculate into the
magno and parvo pathways that feed into the lower inner
part of the visual cortex of the brain. There the sequences of
brightness stimulations are analyzed for movement, and the
movement information is fed directly to the middle temporal
lobe of the brain as the same brightness information is fed
into the outer layers of the visual cortex for analysis of depth.
Simultaneously, signals from the parvo cells of the lateral
geniculate are sorted in the primary visual cortex for color
and form and sent on to the outer layers for further processing.
The outer layers of the visual cortex process information about
depth, form, and color, and feed that information into the
middle temporal area (and other areas) presumably to be associated with the motion information that has arrived by a
different path. Thus the system extracts information about
the motion, position, form, and color of everything in its view
from the few light rays that enter the eye through the pupil.
This information forms a veridical basis for an understanding
of the world outside.

By describing in some detail the structure and function of
the primate visual system, Livingstone and Hubel have laid
the ground work for interpreting psychophysical investiga

tions both past and present. They have described a visual system that processes motion separately from, and more quickly than, form. In doing so, they underpin the conclusions drawn by Kolers two decades before. Working with J. R. Pomerantz, Kolers presented circles and squares in various combinations of apparent motion. He discovered was that the visual system does not hesitate to metamorphose a circle into a square or vice versa in order to preserve the perception of motion in an apparent motion display. To Kolers this readiness to sacrifice form to motion demonstrated that "contour is a relatively late aspect in the construction of visual perceptions, that its formation is plastic, and that it plays a dependent rather than an independent role in figural processes."[19] The psychophysical observations regarding the primacy of motion in humans made by Kolers and Pomerantz are therefore confirmed by the neurophysiological research with macaque monkeys done by Livingstone and Hubel. That independent researchers, working with different methodologies, arrive at similar conclusions, as in this case, is testament to the value of the cooperative enterprise of cognitive science.

Depth

Knowing where things are in three-dimensional space is almost as useful to us today as it was during the long period of our evolutionary development. We have only to cross a busy street to realize that our lives literally depend upon our capacity to locate objects accurately in space. Fortunately, we are very good at it. Our ancestors lived or died on the basis of their ability to know what occupied the space around them. As defenders, they heard the sound of an approaching enemy and, automatically computing the differences in the inputs to their stereophonic ears, turned their heads in the direction of the approaching danger. Having done so, they found themselves facing the enemy and in position to use the visual system. Through their ability to effortlessly compute projective lines of perspective and relative sizes, object overlaps, and the relative changes between objects as they moved their heads, they could track the enemy as he approached. When he was within a few feet, they used their stereoptic capacity to compare the differences in the views from their two eyes to judge precisely where to aim their attack. As hunters, they used the same multi-track system to fix their prey. Indeed, locating objects in space was so fundamentally important that multiple systems developed that served that function.

The most precise locator is *stereopsis*, which takes advantage of the overlapping fields of vision of the two eyes and utilizes the horizontal distance between the eyes and the resulting disparity between the images seen by each. The limitation of this capacity is that it is useful only at close range, for the eyes are placed so close together that after about fifteen feet the view from each eye is so similar there is little disparity to compare. But at close range there is no perception of depth that is so compelling.

The physiological correlates of this effect were first discovered by Hubel and Wiesel thirty years ago in their research on the visual system of cats, and have been elaborated more recently by Livingstone and Hubel working with monkeys.[20] They found in the outer layer of the visual cortex (visual area 2) cells that required stimulation from both eyes, cells that responded to precise degrees of disparity of retinal stimulation.[21] Their findings are consistent with those from a number of psychophysical studies carried out by Bela Julesz at the Bell Telephone Laboratories and reported in his 1971 book entitled *Foundations of Cyclopean Perception*.

Stereopsis is a mechanism of perception that has been studied extensively and well described by these researchers utilizing the methods of neurophysiology and psychophysics. Knowledge of the mechanism of stereopsis has, however, found only limited application in motion pictures. Efforts to market motion pictures utilizing the stereoptic illusion have been largely unsuccessful. And although it is seldom clear why people buy tickets to one movie and not another, the explanation, apart from the awkwardness of wearing the red and green or polarized glasses, seems to be that the image lacks a sense of reality. It appears artificial. Its artificiality would presumably undercut the impact of a serious dramatic picture, so it has been employed mainly for novelty genre movies. Anyone who has been to a three-dimensional movie can report that the people and objects in the movie, while seeming to stand out in space in front of the background, nevertheless seem strangely flattened. And when moviegoers move their heads to the side, instead of gaining a view of the side of the three-dimensional image they see the whole object move with their head movement, as though the objects were following them. Within the illusion of depth created by presenting two images that were photographed simultaneously from slightly different angles, are embedded two other illusions—one, the flattening or "cardboarding" of objects, and two, the movement of the image in response to head movement.

Actually, Julesz solved the first problem, cardboarding, in a practical way. He created a stereogram composed entirely of random dots. Some of the dots were systematically shifted to one side or the other in each of the pair of images such that, although undetectable by one eye alone, the dots formed a three dimensional object when viewed with both eyes, that is, with one eye viewing one of the pair of images and the other eye the other image. Upon viewing the stereograms, one perceived a three dimensional object with rounded contours such as a sphere or ellipsoid. The solution to the "cardboarding" was to avoid any hard edges in the images and place the tiny dots in a point-by-point offset to each other over the surface of the two images. The visual system processes stereoptic depth on a point-by-point basis, and therefore the dotted stereogram met the minimum stimulus requirements to trigger stereoptic depth processing. There was no other information in the brightness array to allow for any other processing.

With the conventional stereoscopic display, such as that of a stereoscope found in an antique store along with a set of double-image photographs or a three-dimensional movie from the fifties, the photographed people and shrubbery have well defined edges. On the card or screen, the variations in depth within the boundaries defined by those edges are ambiguous relative to the clarity of the edges.

It is a curious but consistent phenomenon that the visual system, and indeed the mind itself, will not tolerate ambiguity for long. Instead, it acts decisively (though not necessarily consciously) to resolve the discrepancy. In stereoptic displacement, ambiguity invokes a processing "rule" that quickly resolves the problem—the rule is that when point-to-point displacement computations have ambiguous results, the spatial position of the entire area within a boundary containing those points is "assumed" to be located at the same distance.

Would knowledge of the rule for resolving spatial ambiguity within a boundary allow us to develop a less artificial three-dimensional motion picture? Perhaps. It would require the presentation of unambiguous point-to-point information and maybe some destruction of contrast at edges. But what about the problem presented by the fact that the illusion follows the spectator when he moves his head?

This one may prove more difficult, for it is a function of the projective geometry inherent in the lenses of the camera and projector. For regular movies, positioning of the viewer someplace other than the location of the camera that recorded the image makes little difference. And the effect of head movement is negligible. James Cutting calls this phenomenon *Gournerie's paradox*: the image appears to change little when logically (and mathematically) it should appear distorted from any view other than that of the camera position.[22]

In a three-dimensional movie, Gournerie's paradox does not hold. The constancy underlying the paradox gives way, probably because the powerful system for processing stereopsis, once engaged, overrides and suppresses all other processing of depth. To the viewer occupying a position other than that of the camera, the distortion of the image becomes apparent, and perhaps distracting or annoying. So far, only laser presentations of three dimensional objects have managed to avoid this problem by presenting a standing wave front rather than a lens-focused image.

As I indicated earlier, we have other means of perceiving depth. Apart from stereopsis, the most compelling is *motion parallax*. We take for granted the process for deriving information from motion parallax since we make use of it every day, but occasionally we become aware of its presence. I remember walking through an old cemetery awed by the presence of so many stone markers from the past and touched by the thought of the reverent devotion of surviving spouses and children who placed them there. I wandered among the monuments searching for the name I would recognize as a departed ancestor, my eyes tracing one carved name and then another. As I moved among the stones in this manner, I became aware that the stone upon which I fixed my gaze stood steadfastly in place as I walked around it, while those closer moved in one direction, and those at a greater distance moved in the opposite direction. The farther removed a stone was from the one upon which my gaze was fixed, the faster it moved across my field of vision. My sense of depth was thus magnified, and the space expanded around me. I was tremendously moved by this silent ballet of ancient weathered stellae. And as I walked, I wiped an eye and realized that my perception of depth within the array persisted unchanged in the one eye that remained open and fixed upon the headstone of my ancestor.

My experience of monocular depth among the tombstones was not an unusual perception. Without thinking about how we accomplish the feat, we see and act upon the monocular perception of depth every day. After all, stereopsis does not provide much information about the position of objects located more than a few feet away. Beyond the distance of a few feet, one eye is about as good as two for perceiving depth.

Just how well we can perceive depth with one eye has been demonstrated experimentally by G. J. F. Smets and colleagues with an ingenious configuration of electronic equipment.[23]

They positioned a viewer in front of a video screen and had him fix an eye upon a spot at the top of the screen. In a parallel situation the experimenters positioned a moveable video camera and focused it upon a point the same distance away as the fixation point of the viewer. The camera looked at objects that were arranged in front of and behind the focused point. The image of the objects appeared on the viewer's video screen. The crucial feature of the experiment was that the viewer had a sensor strapped around his head which was connected to the camera in such a way that the camera exactly duplicated his head movements. In other words, when the viewer moved his head the camera moved in precisely the same way.

The reported results are striking: Without the head sensor, and therefore with no control over the image, a viewer saw the kind of limited depth we are accustomed to seeing on a television screen. With the head movement sensor, the viewer had quite a different perception. "Objects positioned before the coincident point were seen as leaping out of the screen. . . . Objects behind the coincident point were seen as if they were behind the screen. . . . The subject had the impression of looking at a rigid, nonmoving scene from different viewing angles. The effect was very strong as long as the camera did follow precisely the subject's head movements."[24]

Smets and his colleagues believe their results support J. J. Gibson's theories concerning movement through a *texture gradient*, the most salient idea being that the information available to the eye of a person moving through an array of textures or objects is sufficient for spatial processing. In Gibson's system, there is no need for logical deduction or informed guesses about the positions of things, and with Smets and his colleagues "no inferential process or mechanisms are supposed."[25] Smets and his colleagues are supported in their avoidance of such supposition by the neurophysiological findings of Livingstone and Hubel that motion and depth processing are carried out by the magno system at lower levels of visual processing.

Once again, an illusion, in the present instance a compelling three-dimensional perception of a video display, has revealed some subtle workings of the visual system. When a situation was constructed in the lab in which the changes in a viewer's head position produced precisely correlated changes in the image on the screen, the information became available to the visual system for making the computations that it ordinarily makes in the real world. The result was a compelling illusion, which is to say that the visual system following its internal rules of processing arrived at a perception that was not veridical, thus revealing the "rules." Apparently, in everyday situations such as my walking among the tombstones, the geometric information available to my eyes is correlated with the precise movement of my head, (and presumably my eyes and body), without any effort or awareness on my part, such that all the computations result in a vivid perception of my exact position in relation to all the objects in my field of view.[26]

As students of the motion picture, we are anxious to understand the implications of the visual system's processing of motion parallax for our processing of space in movies, but let us first consider another perceptual phenomenon—linear convergence or *perspective*. It is an understatement to say that considerable controversy has ensued since the time of Plato as to whether perspective, as employed in drawing and painting and now photography and motion pictures, is a natural function of the eye or an arbitrary, distorting convention of culture. Erwin Panofsky in *Perspective as Symbolic Form* has described two theoretical positions from which attacks upon a naturalist position might be launched:

It is now clear that the perspective view of space (not merely perspective construction) could be attacked from two quite different sides: if Plato condemned it in its modest beginnings because it distorts the "true sizes" of things and puts subjective appearance and caprice in the place of reality

and law, the ultra-modern criticism of art makes exactly the opposite charge that it is the product of a
narrow and narrowing rationalism.[27]

For the film scholar, there is the added burden that the
camera (specifically its lens), embodies the principles for
transforming images by the rules of projective geometry. If
one wishes to assume that perspective is merely a cultural
convention, then one might argue as Jean-Louis Baudry and
others have that the very lens itself is such a convention: that
it was a self-serving invention of quattrocento culture; that it
grew out of the fifteenth century need to rationalize every
aspect of the world; that in the grinding of the glass, not only
the focal length is set but also the ideology of the Renaissance
itself.[28] For Baudry and others, the modern motion picture
had its roots in Renaissance easel painting, and the social,
economic, and political assumptions of Renaissance Italy (and
by extension the Western world) were therefore embedded in
the cinematic apparatus itself. They argued that the perspective in the image, the very construction of the lens itself,
served to perpetuate the ideology of Western culture, and that
the individual film spectator, in the very act of viewing a
film, is of necessity the hapless victim of distortions of capi-
talist ideology.[29]

An alternative view is that even though the lens may have
been developed in the fifteenth century, it is not necessarily
bound to or by Renaissance culture. It is more closely related
to the eye, which has employed such a lens since long before
the Renaissance. And because evolution has given us a lens
which utilizes the principles of projective geometry, it is reasonable to expect that evolution may have also given us the
capacity to extract veridical information about the world from
the "distorted" transformations brought about through the
projective geometry of that lens. In other words, perspective
may not be merely a cultural convention, it may be a built-in
feature of the way we see.

Livingstone and Hubel employed Gibson's corridor illusion

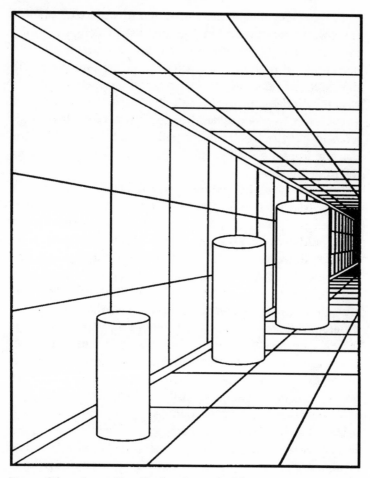

Fig. 4. Gibson's corridor illusion. James J. Gibson. *The Perception of the Visual World.* Copyright © 1950 by Houghton Mifflin Company. Reprinted with permission.

in an experiment that sheds considerable light upon the issue of perspective (see fig. 4). Having discovered during their years of neurophysiological research on monkeys that the visual system consists of two distinct systems, which they called the magno and the parvo, they carried out a number of psychophysical studies with humans.

The corridor illusion results from a line drawing of a corridor with perspectival convergence. Placed along the wall of the corridor are three upright cylinders of equal height. The perceptual illusion is of a corridor receding into space with the three cylinders appearing to be of *different* heights, the closest cylinder appearing smallest and the other two successively larger in order of depth. The illusion of depth and differences in cylinder size is compelling even though we know that the lines are flat on the page and that the cylinders are the same height.

From their earlier neurophysiological finding that the magno system is color blind and responds on the basis of brightness differences, Livingstone and Hubel reasoned that they could deny access to the magno system by rendering the corridor drawing in colors of equal brightness (colors that if photographed in black and white would appear the same shade of gray). In the color version, the lines of the corridor and the outlines of the cylinders became the edges where different colored areas met. The lines of the corridor and cylinders were now defined only by color differences, but they were clearly recognizable nevertheless. When presented with the color version of the corridor illusion, people saw a flat image with cylinders of equal height. The illusion of depth and size difference had disappeared. Livingstone and Hubel reasoned that "if you see depth because you merely know that converging lines mean increasing distance, you should be able to perceive depth from converging lines at equiluminance."[30] In other words, if the illusion of perspective is a matter of learning or convention the subjects should have been able to see depth in the color version just as they did in the line drawing.

Since subjects saw no illusion of depth in the color version but did see depth in the line drawing, Livingstone and Hubel concluded that the illusion of depth from perspective takes place in the magno system, to which the color information is unavailable: "Thus at a relatively low level in the visual system some simple interactions must initiate the automatic interpretation of a two dimensional image into three-dimensional information."[31] The clear implication is that the mere presence of converging lines is sufficient to trigger the processing of depth in the magno system. The internal program, the "rule," is that converging lines recede in depth, in the direction of the convergence. Perhaps the rule implies that in seeking a veridical perception of the world, the visual system has incorporated the rules of projective geometry, a set of computations analogous in this instance to the very rationalism that conventionalists have so feared.

Color

Electromagnetic radiation is the propagation of energy through space. By means of technology we are able to utilize a good portion of the spectrum of that radiation for obtaining and transmitting information. However, we can directly perceive only a small portion of the spectrum. One band of energy can be felt directly on our skin (as heat). An even narrower band can be processed by the rods and cones of our eyes (light).

The further division of light into a color spectrum has been available to vision, in the rainbow, as long as there have been creatures with eyes. The colors of the rainbow always appear in the same order, red, orange, yellow, green, blue, indigo, and violet, from top to bottom. About three hundred years ago Sir Isaac Newton passed a beam of light through a prism and observed that a specific color appeared at each angle of refraction. Passing a beam of light through any glass separates the various wavelengths because the glass transmits the different wavelengths of light unevenly, that is, the shorter wavelengths of blue are bent more than the longer wavelengths of red. (This presents a problem in lensmaking called chromatic aberration.) By using a prism, Newton took advantage of the varying thickness inherent in its shape to exaggerate the chromatic separation. Roughly two hundred years ago the English physician and physicist, Thomas Young, looked at the other half of the interface, the human viewer, and proposed that there are three types of sensors in the eye: one sensitive to red light, one to green light, and one to blue light. The combined ideas that visible light is composed of divisible bands of light that can be distinguished from each other by three different kinds of receptors in the eye, along with the precise psychophysical measurements, is called the Young-Helmholtz theory of color.

If one were to design a machine to interface with an eye that has sensors for red, green, and blue, it would make sense to have the machine produce precisely those wavelengths of light. This is exactly what happened with the development of color television. In the back of a color television set are three electron guns that emit (through a set of filters) red, green, and blue light, or in the jargon of television, *RGB*.

In motion picture film the principle is essentially the same. There are some additional steps in that the camera film must employ filters layered into the emulsion in order to record the various wavelengths separately. (This process is usually referred to as *subtractive*.) But when the finished film is threaded into the projector and the colors are projected upon the screen, the process (additive) and effect are essentially the same as that employed in television.

A three-color theory of color has worked very well for film and television. Such a theory has allowed us to build devices that interface successfully with the human visual system, but it has not been able to account completely for color vision. For example, when the blue and green guns of our television set fire together, to produce blue and green light at the same time in the same place, we see blue-green, which seems intuitively correct. We could have predicted that mixing blue light and green light would have yielded the perception of blue-green light. But what happens if the red gun is fired along with the green gun, and red and green light are projected upon the screen at the same time and in the same position? We might guess that the red light and the green light would combine to produce a kind of greyish or brownish color as if we were mixing colors from a water color set. Instead, what happens where the red and green overlap on the screen is surprising; we see a bright clear yellow.

The perception of yellow under these circumstances is very difficult to account for. The RGB system has proven theoretically sound enough to allow for the development of both color film and television. Why does it not make sense for human perception? For a theorist, this is an exciting development, for what we have is an instance where a reigning theory does not account for all the available data. It is time to question the theory. The yellow of our example is simply not accounted for by the three-color Young-Helmholtz theory of color.

Faced with this dilemma, Hurvich and Jameson proposed another theory.[32] They suggested that perhaps there are receptors in the human visual system that are sensitive to red-and-green and yellow-and-blue. More precisely, perhaps the red and green receptors are paired in a way that requires that they mutually inhibit each other, and the blue and yellow are paired similarly. In other words, receptors could respond to either red or green but not both, and to yellow or blue but not both at the same time. Thus, red is the opponent of green and yellow the opponent of blue. This formulation is known as the *Hurvich-Jameson opponent colors theory.* The perception of yellow as a result of viewing a mixture of projected red and green light is explained in this way: The red light activates the red and yellow receptors, and the green light activates the green receptors. The red and green receptors so activated mutually inhibit each other, in effect cancelling each other, and the activated yellow receptors inhibit the blue receptors. Because there is no activation of the blue receptors to inhibit the yellow, the resulting percept is yellow.

Such a theory can account for the fact that projected red and green light appear to us as yellow light, but it fails to account for yet another aspect of color perception. A one-to-one correspondence does not exist between the wavelength of the incoming light and the color perceived. There are at least three facets of human color perception that attest to this fact.

1) Two patches of the same color can appear different depending upon the color of the background against which they are displayed. 2) Conversely, two patches of the same color can appear to be the same when displayed against carefully selected backgrounds, as Joseph Albers demonstrated in his "Homage to a Square" series. 3) When we walk from outdoors to indoors, from sunlight into shade, or vice-versa, the color of our clothing, the complexion of our skin, and the color of objects surrounding us stay pretty much the same to our eyes. This common phenomenon is called *color constancy*.

As those involved in photography know, no such constancy holds when using color film. Color sensitive film that will render objects in near perfect color outdoors will result in a strange reddish photograph when shot indoors under incandescent or tungsten light. And indoor film, which works fine with 3,200-degree tungsten light, turns everything blue outdoors.

Early video cameras had the same problem. They could not adjust to changes in color temperature. The *white balance* had to be adjusted manually with the camera operators making the judgment as to the setting using their own eyes as a guide. Newer cameras have an automatic "white balance" feature that adjusts for changes in the color temperature of the light.

Edwin Land proposed a theory of color that seems to account for color constancy and in addition explains how the same colors can appear different against different backgrounds or different colors can appear the same.[33] (It also accounts for the perception of yellow from projected red and green light.) The major tenets of Land's theory are the following: First, that accurate perceptions of color result in complex (not isolated) situations in the world. That is, color as perceived in nature is seldom isolated—an array of color usually exists. Second, he distinguishes between brightness and lightness. (Brightness means the amount of light reflected from a surface, and lightness the placement of such a surface on a continuum from white to black.) Third, that the visual system during processing keeps separate the readings from long-wave, medium-wave, and short-wave (red, green and blue) receptors. Fourth, that the way the visual system computes color is by rank ordering input in terms of lightness in three different systems (red, green, and blue), and that the comparison of this ordering results in the perception of a color. For example, a retinal stimulation that would be ranked first in the long-wave system, second in the middle wave system, and last in the short-wave system would be experienced as yellow. Land has gone so far as to develop a method of measuring and comparing brightnesses in a field that accurately predicts the color perception that a person will experience under a wide range of lighting conditions. Land has demonstrated that the process of assigning color is not a matter of cultural convention employing learning or judgment, but rather computation.

5
Sound and Image

Motion, form, depth, and color are, of course, visual phenomena, and considerable attention has been paid them, for just as the sense of olfaction is probably dominant in the canine sensorium, vision is the dominant sense in human perception. Nevertheless, the motion picture medium is bimodal; we *see* and *hear* the events that take place in its space and time. And those who have made movies may have observed that audiences are more tolerant of glitches in the picture than in the sound track. It may seem paradoxical, but our sense systems are so constructed that even though vision tends to dominate sensory disputes, as in "seeing is believing," a break in visual flow is usually less noticeable than a break in the stream of sound. This is not so surprising when we realize that we have lids on our eyes that we blink frequently, usually without awareness, but we have no parallel anatomical structure for our ears. Indeed, our ears are always open and especially attuned to abrupt changes in the sonic flow. In a motion picture sound track, any element that stands out from the flow, any false note, any effect that does not ring true, any interruption sets off an internal alarm that something is wrong. Sometimes the filmmaker can use this characteristic of the auditory system to advantage, but it can just as easily work against the credibility of the film itself. In my production classes, I have told students that sound is seventy percent of the illusion of reality in a motion picture. I am not sure of the number, but my point was, and is, that sound is an extremely important component in the overall illusion of the motion picture. What is so intriguing about motion picture sound is that although motion pictures are shot and edited *double system*, that is, the picture and sound are intentionally kept separate during the production and post production stages of construction, and the projection and sound reproduction technologies are also quite separate in the theater, there is nevertheless an astonishing interaction between sound and image in the spectator's perception.

What the spectator is experiencing is, of course, an illusion of moving figures on a reflective screen interacting with illusions of those figures' voices and their footsteps and the rustling of their clothes and the music from an unseen orchestra. These are illusions interacting with illusions. If we want to know how they interact and how they confer meaning on the events and relationships of the fictional world they inhabit, we must come to know in a way that has some substance, that is nonarbitrary, that has some basis in fact, that squares with reality. To do any less is to create another set of illusions, a parallel fiction that is at best an interesting metaphor but not an explanation.

Why do voices in a movie seem to come directly out of the mouths of the characters, when we know they really come from electric speakers scattered around the theater? Why do contrived sound effects often seem more plausible than the actual effects originally recorded on the production track? Why are we willing to accept, as an integral part of the movie, music that does not have a source in the image on the screen? And why do we like a silent movie better with a musical accompaniment?

Synchrony

The starting point for scientific investigation is direct observation. Much light, for instance, has been shed on the questions posed above by observing human infants. Why infants? Because with adults we cannot be sure whether a particular tendency or stratagem, or program if you will, has been given to us by evolution or by culture. Infants have not had time to acquire much culture. They do what they do spontaneously because of the way they are constructed. They arrive, com-

posite replicas of their progenitors, with programs for interfacing with the world "hard wired" by evolution.

So what have we learned from research with infants that
could tell us something about film viewing? Perhaps the most
important thing is that perception itself is not a passive process. Even for infants, perception is not a matter of seeing
and hearing but rather of watching and listening. As part
of his introduction to a Neonate Cognition Symposium he
chaired at the Twelfth Annual Conference of the Cognitive
Science Society, Richard Held made the following observation:

> Advances in experimental technique and technology
> reveal more and more hitherto unexpected cognitive
> capabilities in infants. Moreover, these achievements
> appear at earlier and earlier ages. We discern a trend
> in infant research as investigators increasingly attrib-
> ute the appearance of cognitive capacity to the devel-
> opment of sensory and motor systems as opposed to
> that of higher centers in the brain. Pushed to an ex-
> treme this trend leads to the view that the neonatal
> mind-brain lacks only the sensory input and motor
> output required to potentiate its capability. In place
> of the *tabula rasa*, organized by sense and movement,
> we would have the neonate *tabula cognitiva* awaiting
> the perfection of its sensory and motor apparatus in
> order to engage the world.[1]

Perception is an information-gathering activity. And when it
occurs in two or more sensory modes simultaneously, it is a
process of information comparison, an active search for cross-
modal confirmation.

When infants are presented with both images and sounds,
they invariably show more interest in the images that link up
with the sounds. Elizabeth Spelke at the University of Penn-
sylvania and Bahrick, Walker, and Neisser at Cornell University, independently conducted a series of experiments on intersensory processing in neonates.[2] Four-month-old infants
were shown films of a game of pattycake, a musical sequence

played on a xylophone, and a slinky moving between two hands. The films were shown two at a time, side by side, but with the sound track for only one of them. The infants spent most of their time (about two-thirds) watching the film that was synced with the sound track.[3]

If simple synchrony between a sound track and an image on the screen is salient to infants, we may reasonably ask, "What about lip sync?" O'Connor and Hermelin presented to ten-week-old infants a mirror image of an experimenter's face as she recited nursery rhymes. In some trials the experimenter's voice was delayed as much as four hundred milliseconds (approximately ten frames). It may come as no surprise that the infants did not spend as much time looking at the experimenter's face in the out-of-sync condition. They watched the act longer in lip sync.[4]

That the infants did not simply revel in the visual and auditory stimulation, but instead actively sought a connection between an unfamiliar sound and an unfamiliar image, suggests that perception is an active process. But how does an infant make the connection between lips and speech, between the sound of a xylophone and the image of a xylophone? Ten-week-old infants have not had time to learn much language, and four-month-olds presumably know little about slinkys and xylophones. How did they make the connection between the sound and the image? The answer is synchrony.

Synchrony serves as a linkage mechanism even at very low levels in the perceptual system. Hummel and Biederman have developed a neural network model for object recognition involving what they call "dynamic binding," a process in which independent features of complex shapes are bound by establishing synchronous firing in the cells representing those features.[5] Temporal synchrony is a basic mechanism for linking sound and image. The processing "rule" may be this: If the auditory and visual events occur at the same time, the sound and image are perceived as one event. Such a conclusion is supported in the work cited here and by many similar experiments with similar results.[6]

Lip sync is a specialized application of the general tendency of our perceptual systems to link sounds and images that occur at the same time. For humans, even very young humans, there is something special about lip sync. We seek speech synchrony, and when we find it, we lock our eyes onto the lips of the speaker and our ears onto the stream of utterances, even if we are too young to have learned the particular language.

We follow the same procedure when watching a motion picture. The fact that the sound actually comes not from the lips on the screen but from a small speaker in the back of the room is not something evolution has prepared us to take into account.[7] Lip sync is so riveting, the cross-modal confirmation of identity of speaker and speech is so compelling, that we apparently ignore any cue that the actual sound energy is emanating from a source other than the mouth of the speaker. This is at least a partial answer to our question about the illusion of the source of speech in a motion picture.

Sound Effects

The insights that perception is an active information-gathering activity and that the mechanism for discerning unity is synchrony also provide a starting point for a discussion of the possibility that a dubbed sound effect can be more plausible than the actual sound recorded on the production track. Suppose for a moment that you are the effects editor for a sequence in a motion picture in which the script says that the footsteps of the killer "resound threateningly in the open stair well." As the editor, you listen to the footsteps as you run the sequence on your flatbed, and you find that they shuffle comically rather than resound threateningly. You take the sequence to a sound studio and ask the Foley artist to create footsteps that "resound threateningly." He does so to your satisfaction, and you cut them into your soundtrack in place of the ones recorded on the set. The result is magic!

When you view the sequence, you have no trouble believing in the authenticity of the footsteps, and now they seem to be a part of the fictional world of the narrative.

That the new footsteps seem to emanate from the moving feet just as convincingly as the old ones did can be explained by synchrony. The threatening footsteps, like the comic ones, are in sync with the image, and synchrony alone is sufficient for the human processing system to link the auditory and visual elements as one event. The question of why the Foleyed steps are more threatening is a different issue. For the Foley artist and the editor, knowing how a sound effect comes to mean something for an audience is not necessary for the production of a compelling effect. Filmmakers can proceed by trial and error, but film theorists, alas, must seek explanations. We must ask whether there are certain patterns of rhythm, pitch, timbre, and onset and offset characteristics universally perceived as threatening, and how much of the feeling of threat is a matter of set and expectation resulting from the dynamics of the narrative itself, and how much proceeds from an acquaintance with general movie conventions.

Elusive as such questions may seem, research in fields that make up cognitive science provides a considerable resource for beginning to answer them. For example, there is a kind of visual stimulus information called *looming*, consisting of continuous and accelerated magnification of a form in the field of view, optical information that specifies collision. The response it provokes is avoidance, retreat, and alarm. Looming is universally perceived as threatening. The response to looming is apparently an innate mechanism.[8]

Other innate mechanisms or strategies for the perception of emotion seem to exist on various levels of human perception. Carroll Izard, Paul Ekman, and Wallace Friesen, among others, have investigated the cross-cultural perception of emotion; and Manfred Clynes has done cross-cultural research on what he calls "sentics," those essential patterns that link sounds, shapes, movements, and music with emotions.[9]

Music

For the present, however, let us return to the issue of synchrony and consider some of the possible relationships of a music track to the picture track. Anyone who has seen a music video has no doubt experienced the hard-hitting effect of cutting the image to the beat of the music. We would explain the perceptual effect as the product of our tendency to link things that occur together—in this case, the cut and the beat. But movies often contain more subtle relationships between music and image. For example, shifts occur in qualities of the music, which coincide with changes in the scene. And during a scene, noticeable patterns emerge that seem evident in both picture and music; if objects or characters are moving rapidly on the screen or events are happening in rapid succession in the film, the music may likewise be moving rapidly or building to a crescendo as the tension in the narrative mounts.

Eleanor Gibson has suggested an explanation for such observations: when we perceive multi-modally, we seek the invariant properties of an event across modalities. Both Eleanor Gibson and J. J. Gibson call them "amodal invariants."[10] Lawrence Marks prefers to call such properties "suprasensory" qualities, but all emphasize that the properties are not modality-specific, but instead constitute information that is carried by all the senses. If patterns and rhythms are confirmed across modalities, the information carried by sound and image is perceived as being generated by a single event.[11]

If such a stratagem exists, it should hold both for sounds and images in the world and for music and pictures in a movie. We have asked how it is that as film viewers we are able to accept music that does not have a source in the image as an integral part of the motion picture. I would suggest that the flow of nondiegetic music might be linked to the flow of the images (and ultimately to the narrative) by our propensity to search for patterns that bridge modalities.

Consider the possibility, too, that the absence of the opportunity to confirm our perceptions cross-modally might account for our discomfort in viewing a silent film without accompaniment. If we are programmed by evolution to check and cross-check our perceptions multi-modally, the inability to do so might well make us fundamentally, vaguely uneasy. The simple addition of musical accompaniment provides a second modality against which to check our impressions and provides confirmation on at least two levels. Musical changes played by the pianist in unison with narrative transitions offer confirmation of the transitions themselves, while the tone and emotion of the music offer confirmation of the event's significance.

The search for cross-modal confirmation most likely occurs simultaneously on several different levels. Perhaps the lowest level of the processes here discussed is that of simple synchrony, checking to be sure that sound and image occur at the same time. At another level, an event of longer duration is checked in both modes for similarity of rhythm and meter. On yet another level, there is comparison of the tone and emotion of the sounds and/or music with the event unfolding on the screen, perhaps the very emotion of the music confirming or denying the validity of the viewer's response to what is seen. And then, perhaps, there is the repetition of a musical motif that has gained particular emotional and narrational significance from its prior use in the film; the motif, along with its many associations, is remembered and both contributes to and serves to confirm the rightness of the viewer's understanding of the implications of the filmic event.[12] If musical and visual information are in conflict in any one of these instances, the conflict will force the viewer to go back and reevaluate earlier reactions, to reinterpret the patterns and the significance of the filmic events.

Similar strategies of cross-modal comparison and correction seem to operate at even the lowest levels of the perceptual system. Albert Bregman explains:

> The correction of one sense by the other has great
> utility.... The human nervous system ... goes back
> and corrects the low level description that is specific
> to each sense organ.... Why should it? Perhaps the
> answer is that the sensory record of an event, say the
> auditory one, is used again by the auditory system in
> combination with other auditory records to compute
> new auditory relations. By going back and correcting
> the raw auditory record and not just the abstract con-
> ceptual one, the brain may guarantee that subsequent
> within-sense computations will be correct.[13]

Eugene Narmour, in the context of his theory of music perception, argues that it is for purposes of this type of "correction of mistakes" that "style shapes," the syntactic primitives
in his model, must be kept separate rather than being totally
assimilated into the schematic style structures of music.[14] Narmour has, in fact, developed a theory of music perception
based upon innate structuring input programs. He writes:
"In short, the Gestalt principles of similarity, proximity and
common direction—as hypothetical constants governing in-
tervallic motion, registral direction, and the elements of
pitch—determine melodic implication without reference to
any preexistent whole and can thus accommodate different
style shapes and different kinds of learned stylistic materials."[15] His implication-realization theory raises many pertinent issues for a cognitive theory of film style.

Just as the visual elements of a film operate as stylistic
factors, so too do the sounds and the music in a film. Film
viewing is a bimodal experience, with the information and
implications carried by each sense mode serving to link and
to group certain sounds and images, to direct attention, to
establish patterns and associations that bring about both
short-term and long-term expectations, and to confirm or deny
the appropriateness of the viewer's response to any given
filmic event.

Summary

We are biological creatures, mammals with well developed sensoria, sensoria that came into being through the processes of evolution in response to the contingencies of survival. In retrospect, it is clear that what survival demanded of perception was veridicality—the truth of the situation from an ecological perspective. We could not afford to be wrong about what was going on around us. We developed discrete senses that carried information along separate pathways. We gained the capacity to check the information being processed by one sensory mode against the information being processed by other modes. This cross-modal checking was apparently so useful that individuals who had a propensity to do so survived when others did not, with the result that to this day human infants are born with the innate tendency to seek cross-modal connections.

I have argued that perception itself is not merely of objects and events but of objects and events with implications. (J. J. Gibson would call such implications "affordances.") Beyond validation of objects and events, the invariant properties perceived across modalities serve to confirm the truth of the perception itself. It must be confirmed or perfected. We cannot afford to be wrong.

Although a movie is an illusion and its content is fiction, we process the illusion of moving figures on the screen and the illusion of their voices and their footsteps and the rustling of their clothes and the music from an unseen orchestra according to a complex set of procedures which employ cross-modal confirmation to ensure veridicality. The power of the motion picture is that its separate streams of images and sounds can be so constructed as to meet the criteria of the perceptual systems, thus eliciting confirmation of the unity and veridicality of *filmic* events.

6
Continuity

While the world in which we live is continuous in both time and space, the shots that make up a motion picture are not. A motion picture is made up of a succession of shots that were perhaps filmed on different days in widely different locations. Even for material that was filmed in the same place on the same day, the camera is started, film is run through the camera and a bit of action is photographed, then the camera is turned off and the film stops. Another bit of action is prepared, the camera is started again, the action is photographed, and the camera is stopped. Each roll of the camera is a *shot*, and at the end of the shooting schedule, hundreds of such shots have been created. The integration of these scores of disparate, disconnected shots is the unique problem of filmmaking and sets it apart from the other arts. It is this "problem," however, which provides the opportunity to structure a film in such a way that when interfaced directly with the human perceptual system through the senses of vision and audition, it functions as a programmed surrogate world—*programmed* in the sense that the filmmaker carefully structures the motion picture to interact directly with the mind of the viewer and *surrogate* in that the mind interacts with the motion picture utilizing the same perceptual system, the same "assumptions" and cognitive procedures that are employed when interacting with the natural environment.

If indeed the problem of integrating a succession of disconnected shots provides the opportunity for the filmmaker to organize these shots in a way that will be precisely meaningful to the viewer, then it is reasonable to ask, How does the viewer perform this integration? But there is a more fundamental question. Since we know that the human perceptual systems were not constructed to interface with motion pictures, but the other way around, how is it that the viewer has the capacity to integrate a succession of views at all?

An adaption or series of adaptions to some environmental pressure (perhaps a food shortage forcing predation) must have instigated the development of the capacity to integrate a succession of views that is now exploited by makers of motion pictures. We know that fishes and frogs and some mammals have eyes on the sides of their heads, positioned for taking in their whole world at once. Theirs is presumably a panoramic view of ever-unfolding events. Other animals, primates in particular, have eyes in the front of their heads that survey a much narrower portion of the environment. As Gibson observed: "This requires turning the head in order to get a full view of the surroundings. Overlapping successive part views had to be substituted for the full view, and the nervous system of the animal had to be adapted to this substitution. The brain had to trade space for time, as it were."[1]

The adaption of the nervous system in humans is such that a succession of partial views results in the perception of a world that is continuous in both space and time. And through a process of trial and error, filmmakers have learned to construct a fictional world on film that, when interfaced with the human perceptual system, is seen by that system as having both spatial and temporal continuity. The final continuity of a motion picture, if it is to be effective, must be foreseen in every phase of its production, the preparation of the shooting script, acting, costumes, and camera positions and moves. In preparing the shooting script, someone (usually the director) must break the action into shots that will "cut" (that is, shots that can later be arranged according to the rules of continuity editing). The director must then shoot for continuity, and the editor must maintain continuity in editing. Clearly, both the director and the editor understand the rules of continuity. Indeed, the rules for maintaining continuity in a classical

Hollywood film are well known; the relationship of these rules to the "rules" by which we process a succession of views in the visual system, however, is not such common knowledge.

We might begin the activity of linking the rules for constructing motion pictures to the "rules" of cognitive processing, by identifying the better understood side of the equation and sorting the conventions of filmic continuity into three categories. Category one contains the "cuts" themselves, the simple shot-to-shot transitions. The task for the editor is to choose a shot that will "cut" with the one immediately preceding it and then to find precisely the right place to end the first shot as well as the exact frame with which to begin the second shot. In carrying out this task, the editor attempts to avoid jump cuts, to change camera angle and image size at every cut, to maintain screen direction, and to meet the requirements for matching action.

Category two consists of sequences of shots that have an orientational relationship to each other, relationships that in the argot of the trade are known as shot-reverse-shots, point-of-view shots (POVs), over-the-shoulder shots (OTSs), and eye-line matches. Here the filmmaker is concerned to make clear the physical orientation of the characters to each other and to their environment, and, of course, he knows the rules for doing so.

Category three is comprised of the large-scale relationships between places and events in the entire diegetic world of the motion picture. Here the dramatic events of the story can leap across time and space. The filmmaker employs the filmic devices of cross-cutting as well as flashbacks or flash-forwards. By means of such devices, parallel actions can erupt and converge, and the Hollywood staple, the chase, becomes possible.

Comparison of the three categories reveals that they are not independent. Quite to the contrary, they can be described as hierarchical or nested, that is, category one is contained within category two, which is in turn contained within category three. Recognition of the nested arrangement of the relationships between a series of shots in a motion picture is

essential to understanding filmic continuity, and I shall return
to this idea momentarily, but first, let me explore each category
in an attempt to connect filmic construction with visual processing. Indeed, how might the rules of construction be related
to the "rules" of processing?

Shot-to-Shot Transitions

Category one contains the perennial enigma for film scholars,
the jump cut. The rule of continuity is simply that such cuts
should be avoided. It is true that sometimes the rule is intentionally violated, and we shall consider the implications of
violation in this discussion. But first, just what is a jump cut,
and why does it jump? A "cut" in film is the point where two
shots are joined, that is, where one shot ends and the next
one begins. The term *jump cut* is commonly used to refer to
any break in continuity, but its origins are in the characteristic
awkward "jump" that sometimes occurs at the transition from
one shot to another. (It can also occur within a shot if a few
frames have been removed.)

Think for a moment about how we use our visual system
in the natural environment. We do not merely look at things;
we look around. We explore, we search with our eyes. We
move our eyes, we turn our heads, we rotate our whole bodies,
and we walk around and among objects in our environment.
All this provides us with different views occurring successively in time. As Gibson has observed: "There is no need to
perceive everything at once if everything can be perceived in
succession."[2]

So what happens, for example, when we view a tree directly
in front of us, then quickly turn our head to view another
tree to our right? Do we have any trouble integrating the two
views? Of course not. We have the veridical perception that
there are two trees, one directly before us and one directly
to our right. We should note, however, that there are at least
two other kinds of information here: 1) as we turn our heads,
we see the intervening ground between the two trees; and 2)

internal feedback indicates that we are turning our heads ninety degrees. Put another way, the visual system "assumes" a stable and continuous world in which objects that exist continue to exist, and the viewing of the ground and the proprioceptive feedback to the visual system verify the fact.

Now suppose that we are looking at a motion picture shot in which the camera pans from the first tree to the second one. Do we have any trouble integrating the view of the first tree with the second? Probably not, for we see the first tree and the ground in between and then the second tree. It is true that we are missing the proprioceptive feedback of our head turn, but in this case, the visual information for our head turn will probably override the proprioceptive information for lack of movement. If such overriding does not occur, we may see the first tree and then the rotation of the *ground* to the second tree. Next, suppose we are watching a film in which a shot of the first tree is followed directly by a shot of the second tree. We may see a "jump" at the transition. Why? Because the "assumption" of a stable and continuous world that is built into the visual system functions the same way in viewing a movie as it does in the natural world. In the absence of any information to the contrary, the visual system makes its computations on the basis of the two trees being the same tree. Since the visual system, along with its processing "rules," developed long before the motion picture, it cannot take the possibilities of motion pictures into account. It therefore sees the tree jump to a new position and different configuration rather than allow that the tree has ceased to exist and been replaced by another (which is exactly what has happened).

In the natural world, trees stand all their lives rooted in one place. They do not jump around. When we see a tree jump, we have certainly seen an illusion. Paradoxically, the tree is seen to jump because the visual system has a built-in "assumption" of a stable world, one in which objects that exist continue to exist. That seems simple enough, but the meaning of "assumption" must be made clear in this context. The reference is *not* to an individual's expectations based upon prior experience with the environment or with watching movies, but instead to a "hard-wired" process developed in the course of the biological evolution of our perceptual systems.

We know (from chap. 4) that the visual system processes motion via the magno system faster than it processes form and color via the parvo system. Motion can be perceived without form and so can apparent motion. The minimum requirement for the perception of motion is that a blob, that is, a patch of light or dark defined by its brightness, achieves displacement relative to its background.[3] It becomes clear at this point that the "assumption" we are talking about resides at a very basic level; no inference or intellectualization occurs. In viewing the tree-to-tree jump cut, we first see a blob jump, and then that what is jumping is a tree, a thing that cannot jump.

Any two contiguous shots containing objects that are so similar as to be taken as the same blob by the visual system are likely to result in a jump cut—for example, a man and a refrigerator, or a button and a bagel. But what about a shot of a man that is cut into two pieces and spliced together with a few frames taken out? Here it is clearly not a matter of identity (it is the same man), but it is still a matter of seeing the blob jump rather than allowing it to cease to exist, even for a fraction of a second.

In practical terms, the removal of just one frame of a moving subject will usually not be noticed, the removal of two will sometimes cause a jump, and cutting out three frames almost always causes jumps. This is the point at which the spatial limit for short range apparent motion has been crossed. Generally with motion pictures, only in a jump cut does the displacement exceed the limits of the fine grain illusion. Perhaps that is why it is so jarring.

In our effort to understand why a jump cut "jumps," we must remember that the processing is occurring at a very basic level in the visual system, at the level of motion processing which takes place in the magno system prior to form processing in the parvo system. (See chap. 3.) And though (in a jump cut) there is sufficient similarity in the pattern of light/dark to indicate to the visual system the continuity of the object (meaning the two blobs are taken for the same blob), the spatial displacement is greater than the usual transition from frame to frame in a motion picture. The conditions are thus met for the illusion of motion that we have previously identified as long-range apparent motion.

Since the "rule" of continuity of existence has been invoked, let me be specific about what is meant. First, the "rule" is hypothetical, but the visual system behaves consistently as though such a rule in fact exists. Second, such a "rule" points out the distinction between the way things actually work physically and the way we perceive things from our ecological perspective. Put another way, we as scientists can discover by various indirect means how things actually work in the universe, but as ecological animals we are limited to what we can perceive directly via our senses. Our senses developed through the evolutionary process to give us information about the world that was veridical, information that we could act upon. Evolution could not have anticipated that we would develop scientific methods that would enable us to explore by indirect measures the fundamental laws of the universe. It is important for us as students of perception to avoid what might be termed the scientific perception fallacy, the error of assuming that our perceptual and cognitive systems arrive at perceptions and understandings by the same procedures and methods that we as scientific investigators employ.

Gibson offered the following example to distinguish between what he called the perspectives of *ecology* and of *physics*: "When a solid substance with a constant shape melts, we say that the object has ceased to exist. This way of speaking is ecological, not physical, for there is physical conservation of matter and mass despite the change from solid to liquid."[4] Our perceptions are therefore veridical from our perspective inside the ecological system; we are well informed about the

events that are likely to affect us, events that occur in our
time and space. Spatially, we can perceive things as small as
a grain of sand or as large as a mountain, and our sense of
time ranges from about a tenth of a second to perhaps three
generations of our family. Outside these boundaries our perception fails us, and we must employ indirect methods in
order to acquire information. Inside the boundaries of our
own time and space, however, we can perceive the world directly. Evolution has equipped us to do so.

The "rule" of continuity of existence inherent in our visual
system holds that objects that exist continue to exist until
they are seen going out of existence. And going out of existence is a fairly rare event and must meet rigorous criteria. It
should not be mistaken for the far more common event of
merely going out of sight. With regard to cessation of existence, Gibson was very explicit and insisted upon distinguishing this phenomenon from simple occlusion: "Going out of
existence, cessation or destruction, is a kind of environmental
event and one that is extremely important to perceive. When
something is burned up, or dissolved, or shattered, it *disappears*. . . . It does not disappear in the way that a thing does
when it becomes hidden or goes around a corner."[5] When
something burns up, dissolves, or shatters we *see* it go out of
existence. Seeing in this instance is believing, and we can act
upon that perception. The information is veridical from an
ecological perspective, if not factual from the perspective of
physics. And it is critically important information: we cannot
afford to be wrong about whether an object has ceased to
exist or has simply gone out of sight. If, for instance, the
leopard of our earlier example merely stepped behind a clump
of bushes and our visual system "assumed" that he had ceased
to exist, we would probably not live long enough to pass on
our faulty genes.

That objects continue to exist even when they are out of
sight, and that objects tend to move as units that cannot move
through space occupied by other objects, are not intellectual
discriminations acquired late in life. Experimental evidence

suggests that infants make these "assumptions."[6] And there is further evidence that the continuity of existence of occluded surfaces is processed at a very low level in the visual system.[7]

The perception of cessation of existence is probably a higher level perceptual activity than perceiving continuity of existence in the presence of temporary occlusion. For example, infants were for a long time thought to lack the ability to perceive continuity of objects when the objects are out of sight. More recent evidence suggests that perhaps infants simply expect an object to reappear in the place where it was last seen. What infants may lack is not the ability to assume continuity but an understanding of the irrevocable nature of entropy. In other words, if something really does go out of existence, infants may not perceive the fact; infants may not know that objects cannot be reconstituted.[8]

Some going-out-of-existence events can be perceived directly as part of our experience of the fictional world of a film, as, for example, when a house burns to the ground, when a swimmer sinks under the water and does not resurface, when a plate glass window shatters, or when someone who is wounded suddenly becomes limp and still. Other going-out-of-existence events are transitional devices that are not part of the illusion but filmic conventions. They function at another level and are metaphorical in nature.

Some such devices are fairly obvious. A fade-out/fade-in is used to connote a passage of time and is analogous to the change from nightfall to morning in the natural world. A dissolve is the going out existence of one scene and the coming into existence of the next. A dissolve is most often used like the fade-out/fade-in to indicate a passage of time or to mark the transition from one state to another, such as from present time to flashback or from present reality to a dream or reverie state. Some of the more complex video effects, such as the fragmentation of one scene and the constitution of the next scene from the fragments, are variations of the going-out-of-existence device. Classification of such filmic devices must be done carefully, however, for they are not of the same order as ordinary cuts, match-action cuts, and jump-cuts.

Taking into account what we know about the "rules" of processing (continuity of existence, rigidity, and occlusion), let us consider how filmmakers have (by trial and error) developed conventions of filmmaking that interface more or less successfully with the visual system. What about a straightforward cut? If the juxtaposition of certain shots creates a jump, then what kinds of shots can be expected to cut together without a jump? The answer is, of course, any two shots that do not violate the rule of continuity of existence. For example, a cut from a tree to a busy downtown intersection or from a pencil to a house is not likely to jump, because they are very different. Shots that are very different from each other tend not to jump when cut together. Let me hasten to say that it is not a matter of the content of a shot. It is because the array of light and dark blobs are so different that the visual system does not process for continuity (that is, the same object), but instead "resets" and starts the computation anew.

Another convention is the so-called invisible cut. The most invisible cut of all is counterintuitive and, on the face of it, would seem the most unlikely candidate. We film an actor in long shot performing an action. Then we stop him, move the camera in closer and to one side, then have him repeat the action. In the editing room, we take the first shot and let it run to the high point of the action; then we physically cut the film right in the middle of the action and splice on the second shot, being careful to start the second shot a couple of frames of action earlier than the place where the action is cut in the first shot. The result is a cut between two shots that is very difficult to perceive. It is practically invisible. We call it a match-action cut.

Let us consider the rules of continuity editing that are employed in a match-action cut and the "rules" of visual processing that are activated in the viewer. The rules of thumb employed on the filmmaking side are four. 1) The angle and image size must be changed between two successive shots. This is called the 30-degree rule because the angle is supposed to be changed by at least 30 degrees. 2) The 180-degree rule must be adhered to so that screen direction remains consistent. If the camera stays on the same side (within 180 degrees) of the axis of principle action, the characters will not change the direction they are moving or facing on the screen. 3) The cut should be made at the point of greatest action. 4) The action (not the actual film) should be overlapped approximately two frames when making the splice.

As we have noted, filmmakers generally do not know why following these rules results in an invisible cut. They simply know that the procedure works. Worse yet, film scholars do not know why the rules of match-action cutting work, but apparently few writers on film have been sufficiently intimidated by their lack of understanding to refrain from adding to the confusion.

In viewing a motion picture, the viewer's position with regard to the people and objects in the scene is the position of the camera. If we place a camera on a tripod across the street from our house and take a shot of the house, then with the camera stopped move it in a straight line toward the house and set it up again on the sidewalk and take a second shot, and later cut these two shots together and look at them projected on a screen, we will see the house "jump" toward us at the cut. Why? Because we have insufficient information for self-movement, either from the visual array or from proprioceptive feedback. And yet the house in the second view is larger than in the first. In the absence of adequate information for self-movement, the system resolves the incongruity by "assuming" continuity of existence: the house must move from its position in the first shot to its position in the second shot. This is an efficient perception of the situation, not by the rules of reason, but by the rules of projective geometry.

Now suppose we had followed the 30-degree rule and had moved the camera to a position on the sidewalk thirty degrees to the right of an imaginary line drawn from the center of the house to the first camera position. In this case when the two shots are projected one sees the house from the first position and then from the second position with a smooth transition at the cut rather than a "jump." Why? Because this time not only the size of the image has changed (as in the previous example), but the projective geometry inherent in the image provides unambiguous information that *we* have changed our position (the camera has changed its position) rather than the house having changed its position.

Our visual system can account for the differences in the appearances of objects as we move around and successively fix our eyes upon things. In the first example, had we quickly dollied the camera from across the street to its second position on the sidewalk or had we merely zoomed from the first shot to the larger view of the second shot we would have seen the transition and there would have been no jump (of course, there would have been only one shot). In the second example, where both the image size and the camera angle is changed, the information from projective geometry for the change of the viewer's position is multiple and corroborative. That information is sufficient for accurate perception of the successive views even in the absence of proprioceptive feedback indicating self-movement.

The fact that the visual system will process a succession of views from different camera positions, without requiring confirmation from proprioceptive feedback that the viewer has *actually* moved from one position to another, makes film editing possible. But the views must be presented in patterns that can be processed by the visual system if the illusion of reality is to be maintained, and the limits of such patterns are reflected in the rules of continuity filmmaking.

Again, the rules applicable to a match-action cut include: 1) the angle and image size must be changed between two successive shots (the 30-degree rule), 2) the 180-degree rule must be followed, 3) the cut should be made at the point of greatest action, and 4) the action (not the actual film) should be overlapped approximately two frames when making the splice. Rule two relates to the fact that if the camera stays on the same side (within a 180-degree arc) of the axis of principle action, the character(s) will not change the direction they are facing or moving on the screen. The concept is straightforward and needs no elaboration except with regard to the direction of movement. Our visual systems operate according to an "assumption" that moving objects will continue to move in the same direction unless we see them change direction. Whether this "assumption" is an innate part of visual processing or learned at a very early age is not presently known, but it holds for actions in the world and for the movies as well.

The third rule mentioned in regard to match-action cutting holds that the cut should be made at the point of greatest action. There is some leeway here, for sometimes the cut can be made just before the action or just after the action, but the rule is related to the "assumption" of the visual system that motion will continue in the same direction at approximately the same speed.

Film editors sometimes attempt to explain a match-action cut by saying that the motion carries the eye through the cut. This is not a bad explanation, but it functions at the level of metaphor, and does not provide a functional mechanism. For a more precise understanding, we must recall that motion is processed very rapidly by the magno system without recourse to form or color processing. To successfully interface with that system, that is, the motion processing system, all the filmmaker need do is join together two shots with similar blobs moving at about the same speed and direction. No wonder a match-action cut works so well; the two shots are perceived as one motion prior to the processing of the forms involved.

The fourth rule, that the action should be overlapped by two frames, makes no intuitive sense at all to film editors, but all the good ones know to do it. Perceptual psychologists, on the other hand, should have no trouble explaining why the overlap is necessary, for a large body of research exists on masking phenomena.[9] Research on masking tells us that

incoming information generally overrides ongoing processing. If we think about it, we realize that the visual system
could not proceed otherwise, for our chances of survival are
surely increased if we can catch the presence of an intruder
quickly in the corner of our eye while we are looking at
something else, or if we can hear a twig break in the darkness over the normal sounds of communal living. Attention
is tuned to the new, to the unusual, to change in our environment. In a motion picture, a new shot simply overrides
(masks) the processing of the last couple of frames of the old
shot. Editors know, from previous experience, that cuts where
the action is perfectly matched do not work very well, and
whether they understand masking or not, they insure that
there will be no gaps in the action presented to our visual
system by simply overlapping the action by approximately
two frames at the cut. (They proceed by trial and error to
find the exact number of frames of overlap needed at a particular cut.)

Orientational Relationships

Category two in our taxonomy of continuity editing consists
of orientational relationships between shots in a sequence,
relationships inherent in shot-reverse-shots, point-of-view
shots (POVs), over-the-shoulder shots (OTSs), and eyeline
matches. Making sense of these combinations of shots depends in large part upon the viewer's correct recognition of
the physical orientation of the characters to each other and
to their environment. A conversation in a restaurant is usually
presented as a category two construction; the orientation of
the characters to each other and to the immediate environment is maintained by carefully positioning the camera so
that viewers can without effort, by relying upon their own
automatic internal computations, use the information provided by the projective geometry inherent in the photographic
image to make sense of the situation. By employing the devices of category two continuity, the filmmaker makes it both

easy and necessary for viewers to comprehend the unfolding event by making the same computations for the diegetic world of the film that they (the viewers) make for the real world.

As noted earlier, the viewers' position with regard to the characters and objects in a scene is the camera's position. This is a truism; we have access to no other position. The computations the viewers make take into account their perspective, that is, the position of the camera as it moves about the characters (though they do not necessarily do so knowingly). The position of the camera simply becomes the starting point for all computations.

Recall, if you will, Gibson's admonition that we do not simply look, we look around with our eyes, our heads, our bodies, and our minds. "Vision is a whole perceptual system, not a channel of sense. . . . One sees the environment not with the eyes but with the eyes-in-head-on-the-body-resting-on-the-ground."[10] Incorporated in our looking around is a sense of our own position in relation to the objects and events we are looking at. While moving around, continually shifting our own position, we are keeping track of where we stand in and amongst the objects we are looking at. Think for a moment. Could it be otherwise? After all, we did not develop as god-like observers of the world, but as participants in its life-and-death struggles. It becomes clear with regard to mammalian evolution that nature could not leave something so important as knowing where one is standing to some higher level intellectual process in which a species of primate might someday develop the capacity to indulge. The capacity to know where one is located had to be primitive, dependable and heritable.

One of the most memorable scenes employing level two continuity is contained in the 1942 movie *Casablanca*. The scene is the one in which Ilsa returns alone to Rick's Cafe after closing time. This scene follows the flashback sequence (not a category two construction) in which Ilsa and Rick's past relationship is depicted. The first shot is an out-of-focus close-up (CU) of a bottle, a glass, and Rick's hand. His hand clumsily knocks over the glass, and the camera reframes to reveal Rick seated at a table. The shot is a medium shot with Rick framed near the right margin of the screen facing screen left. Unfortunately, the shot that follows is also a medium shot, but with Rick framed at the left edge of the screen sitting, staring blankly across the table. Therefore, the transition from the first shot to the second is very awkward and results in a change of screen direction (a category one continuity problem). Fortunately, what follows this clumsy beginning is a carefully articulated series of shots held together in the viewer's perception through the forces triggered by the director/editor's employment of the devices of category two continuity. The camera dollies back to a long shot (LS) as Sam enters the frame from the left, crosses the frame behind Rick and the table, and from the right edge of the frame reaches out and sets the overturned glass aright. He then picks up a chair from the floor and places it at the table directly across from Rick. From the camera's position, the viewer looks across the table and into the background at the door to the street. The door opens and Ilsa crosses the threshold and stands framed in the light of the doorway. Rick moves his head to look in her direction (point glance). Cut to CU of Rick looking in the direction of the door (glance continued). Cut to CU of Ilsa, her eyes fixed intently upon Rick (eyeline match across room) as she closes the door behind her. Cut to CU of Rick (eyeline match) his gaze still fixed upon Ilsa. He stops the pouring action he has begun and sets down the bottle. Cut to LS (same as opening shot) with Rick still seated at the table and Ilsa deep in the entryway. With her eyes still fixed upon Rick, she walks forward toward the table (and the camera). "Rick, I have to talk to you." Rick responds sarcastically, "I saved my first drink to have with you," as he pushes the bottle toward her. She declines his offer and sits down. The camera moves in closer and reframes. The result is a two shot that favors Ilsa (that is, the camera is positioned nearer Rick providing an image of him from the side and Ilsa in three-quarter view). Their exchange continues, ending with her line "I didn't count the days." Cut to OTS (her shoulder) of Rick. "I did, every one of them." As Rick finishes, there is a cut back to the two-shot that now functions in this pattern of shots as an OTS (his shoulder) of Ilsa. He downs his drink. She asks to tell her story, and some verbal sparring ensues. At this point the OTSs are abandoned and there is a cut to a CU of Rick. "Go ahead and tell it." Cut to a CU (reverse shot) of Ilsa, who begins telling her story. Cut to a CU (reverse shot) of Rick, who begins with "Yes, that's very pretty...," and continues with biting sarcasm. Cut to CU of Ilsa listening, obviously wounded. Cut to CU (reverse shot) of Rick, who begins "Tell me..." Cut to CU (reverse shot) of Ilsa's reaction as he continues, "Who was it you left me for?" Cut to CU of Rick (reverse shot) as he finishes his stinging line, "Or aren't you the kind that tells?" Cut to CU of Ilsa (reverse shot), who lowers her eyes in disgust, giving up on trying to talk to Rick. She starts to stand. Cut back to the original long shot. Ilsa rises from the table and walks toward the door without looking back. Rick in the foreground slugs down a drink. Cut to CU of Rick (head-on). He buries his face in his hands and falls forward on the table. The camera moves in on the crumpled heap. Fade to black.

The shot-reverse-shot pattern is not merely a device of post-production editing; it requires careful placement of the camera for its initial production. The first shot in such a series requires that the camera be placed so that the characters can be seen together in one shot and their spatial relationship clearly established. The next two shots are usually OTSs, over the shoulder of first one of the characters and then the other, followed by two or more alternating close-ups. One might ask the purpose of the OTSs; why not go directly to close-ups, on the basis that the relative positions of the characters has been established? In the *Casablanca* scene, we know that Rick and Ilsa are seated across the table from each other. Of course one can cut directly to the close-up, but the viewer is then denied both the feeling of intimacy such shots convey and the information that is contained in the perspective of the OTSs. In other words, the OTSs provide a projective geometry with which viewers can further refine their computations as to the relative positions of the characters.

The computations viewers make in this circumstance are not high level or inferential, they are merely the automatic computations that are normally made on the basis of information from the projective geometry inherent in lensed images. The projection is, of course, to the position of the camera, but in this instance that is the position from which all calculations must be made. The position of the camera becomes the position of the viewer for purposes of computation by the simple expediency of available information (that is, the information that is available from projective geometry is referenced to that point.)

Let us return to the close-ups in the shot-reverse-shot pattern. One may observe that the CUs are shot from the same camera angle as the OTSs, and one may ask why they are not shot from the positions of the characters themselves. The answer may seem simplistic, but it is extremely important for our understanding of the orientational nature of category two continuity constructions. If the first CU of Ilsa were shot from Rick's position, Ilsa would be looking right into the lens of the camera. If that were allowed to happen, the eyeline match that had been established and carefully preserved between Ilsa and Rick would be broken and replaced with an eyeline match between her and every member of the audience. The idea may be titillating, but the scene would be destroyed. As Edward Branigan has observed: "A look into the camera breaks the diegesis because it makes the conventional reverse shot or eyeline match impossible. (Such a match would reveal the camera itself; its absence would be just as revealing.)"[11] This is, of course, why actors are generally instructed not to look at the camera, but it is even more significant in a category two construction of continuity because here the terms of the realization of the scene are vested in the orientations of the characters toward each other.

Hierarchical Spatial Comprehension

There are also filmic constructions of continuity that go beyond the eyeline matches and shot-reverse-shot patterns of category two. There are constructions, which we may call category three constructions, that do not rely solely upon the viewer's capacity to use the information contained in the projective geometry inherent in the photographic image. They provide viewers with information for comprehending the entire diegetic world of the movie even though that world is never seen altogether in one shot from one perspective.

It turns out that humans have a specialized capacity, a neurophysiological mechanism, probably located in or at least coordinated by the hippocampus in the brain, which allows for such comprehension in both movies and the world: "The spatial cognitive system . . . has several intriguing characteristics. First, it operates on a domain that has a clearly nested structure. . . . Second, the system stores information about the spatial domain in a way that captures that hierarchical structure very effectively. . . . Third, the system enables us to 'mentally revisit' places that we have once encountered without actually returning to them."[12]

A motion picture such as *Casablanca* is, in a sense, a program that activates the viewer's capacity for complex spatial comprehension. Naturally and with minimal effort, the viewer maps out a city with an airport, a police station, a hotel, a place called the Blue Parrot, and of course, Rick's Cafe. The city is Casablanca, which is in French Morocco, which is on the North Coast of Africa, which is part of a roundabout path from Paris to Lisbon, which are cities in France and Portugal in Western Europe. All is comprehensible because in movies, as in the world, Gibson's observation holds true: "A place can be located by its inclusion in a larger place."[13]

At the local level, our "cognitive map" of the fictional Casablanca places Rick's Cafe near the airport.[14] We are therefore not surprised when Rick, Ilsa, and Victor with the police chief in tow arrive quickly at the airport from the cafe, while Major Strasser races through traffic from the offices of the German Commission of Armistice only to arrive after the plane, carrying Ilsa and her husband to freedom, has already taxied away from the terminal. The cross-cutting that begins with Louis's phone call to Strasser from Rick's Cafe and ends with Strasser's arrival at the airport terminal building is an example of category three filmic continuity. Cross-cutting relies upon an overall comprehension of three-dimensional space that is not tied to any particular visual perspective, that is, to a specific camera position or succession of camera positions, as in shot-reverse-shot sequences of category two constructions. Category three constructions are not directly dependent upon camera position; they depend instead upon the viewer's capacity to recognize a hierarchical spatial pattern, a gestalt of places nested within places.

By separating conventional Hollywood continuity into three categories, I have attempted to show how each interfaces with specific perceptual capacities of the human mind. Indeed, the wide accessibility of the classical Hollywood film rests in no small part upon the discovery and subsequent incorporation into convention of a number of rules for filmic construction that allow the film to interact directly with the human perceptual system.

One can, of course, structure a motion picture in ways other than by the rules of continuity, and a filmmaker may have good reasons for employing some other set of conventions. But a filmmaker should understand that a movie, in which successive shots are not presented in such a way that they can be processed directly by the visual system and integrated into a continuous flow of time and space, must be grasped indirectly at the level of symbol and metaphor. Such a movie is likely to be comprehensible only within the confines of its own culture or perhaps to those familiar with the particular filmic conventions.

In contrast, the conventions of continuity, developed through trial and error over a period of almost a century, have resulted in a set of rules for presentation of images that are compatible with the "rules" of processing of the human visual system. The implication is that continuity shooting and editing is a set of programming rules for transforming a series of shots into a surrogate environment. Pictorial continuity is not bound by the culture that developed it. It is not necessarily an expression of that culture's ideology. Apart from any specific content, it can be appropriated by anyone for any purpose.

7
Diegesis

We sit in a darkened theater, our gaze fixed upon the invisible screen, and out of the darkness a star-filled sky appears before us. We feel a floating sensation as we futilely try to fix the points of light in a void of pure lapis lazuli. Our view tilts slightly downward to reveal a bright horizon. We are somehow comforted by the sight of the horizon. Suddenly from over our right shoulder a star ship blasts its way into the void, leaving us looking into its rear rocket thrusters as it rapidly recedes into the distance. A deep rumbling surrounds us, and we become aware of a great presence, its wedge-shaped nose piercing the space before us, its sleek grey belly sliding over our heads, filling our vision, triggering a sudden rush of mortal panic. Goosebumps rise, and hairs stand outward from our flesh, for we have arrived "a long time ago in a galaxy far, far away."

What is this magic that is a movie? How do we enter into its space, its time?

The short answer is that we enter directly in a way that is neither abstract, nor intellectual, nor linguistically based. A motion picture engages our capacity to participate in the diegesis through its capacity to present surrogate arrays to our visual and auditory systems, and at another level but nested within the first, through its capacity to present characters interacting in a time and place.[1] On the viewer's side, entry into the fictional world occurs through our capacity to process the light from the screen and the sound from the speakers exactly as we process all ambient arrays of light and all disturbances of the molecules of the air in which we swim, coupled with our capacity to pretend and to set apart special activities from the normal flow of events in the world—that is, to frame.

Visual Orientation

We enter the fictional world of *Star Wars* viscerally, small and vulnerable and disoriented, peering into the void, floating in space above the surface of a planet. We enter effortlessly as though being pulled by an unseen force into the void, pulled not by intellectual inference or verbal persuasion, but by the optic and auditory arrays that affect our perception most directly.

Knowing where we are is so basic to our survival, so fundamental to our perception, that we are uncomfortable with disorientation, and we panic when we are lost. The senses, especially vision and audition, work together with proprioceptive systems to provide a veridical perception of where we are at all times. The movements of our eyes, our head, and our body are continually fed back through proprioception to facilitate ongoing computation of our position. The fluid contained in the semicircular canals of our ears continually adjusts to gravity, and the position of the liquid against the sensors in the canals continually signals our orientation with regard to gravity. All these systems work together to help us know where we are.

A great deal of research has been done on proprioception and orientation, and the major outcome, at least for our purpose, is that invariably when one of these systems is set in conflict with vision, it is vision that dominates.[2] Visual motion can make us seasick, visual distortions of verticality and horizontality can make us stumble, and the appropriate visual information in a movie can make us feel that we are floating in space. Only because vision dominates proprioception is it possible for a motion picture to provide the information for self-movement. Only because the visual array provides compelling information to the visual system for changes of viewer position is it possible for us to integrate a succession of shots from several different camera positions into one unified visual inspection of the scene. Likewise, it is only because information in the visual array is given priority in perception that it is possible to enter the diegetic space of a motion picture effortlessly by way of the visual system without the necessity of proprioceptive confirmation. And only because the visual system gives us such a visceral sense of where we are, does our presence in the fictional world of the motion picture seem so real.[3]

The Capacity to Play

If the "rules" of visual and auditory processing allow for the illusion that we are surrounded by the diegetic space, there is yet another set of "rules" that allows us to sustain the illusion of the reality of a motion picture's fictional world. Actually, both the capacity of the visual system to process a synthetic array of light as reality, and the capacity of the mind to pretend, allow access to the motion picture. The first allows direct access to the fictional *world* and the second direct access to the *fictional*.

The capacity to pretend, to set apart certain of our activities as having special status (framing), is a part of *play*, and as such it is available to all of us at all ages. Among humans it is pervasive; it is universal. Nor is it limited to our own species.

I first became aware of the widespread access to play years ago as my two small sons, our dog Sophie, and I played a game on the living room floor. Actually it was Sophie's game; she taught it to us. We would arrange ourselves in a circle with Sophie taking the lead. She would stretch her forepaws forward and place her chin upon them while her rear haunches were elevated with her tail sticking straight up and constantly wagging. She would make short lunges at us, baring and snapping her long white teeth and making short frequent yipping sounds all the while. We assumed her position as best we could considering the differences in anatomy and did likewise, except that for some reason we tended to grab at her with our hands rather than nip with our teeth. We all had great fun attacking and retreating in mock ferocity. We would grab her but let her go; she would take our arms in her mouth but never bite hard enough to break the skin. All of us, a university professor, two children, and a very bright dog (but a dog nevertheless), knew that we were playing a game. We each had the capacity to frame the activity as being special, outside the normal flow of events. The forepaws and head down, the wagging tail, and the short, high-pitched yips all signaled that we were playing a game. We were engaged in pretending that we were fighting, but we knew we were playing. Was our knowing, our framing of the activity, an abstract, an intellectual, or a linguistically based achievement? Hardly, the whole idea was Sophie's.

Playfulness, the predisposition to play, is a heritable trait. Our capacity to play, to say "Let's pretend" and enter into another (avowedly illusory or fictional) world, is one of our programs. It is given to us by biology, through the process of evolution, and it is not too difficult to imagine how or in what way it had survival value.

The mode of "Let's pretend" allows individuals in a species to try out behavior without the consequences of the real situation. For example, a young animal can learn the moves for attack and defense in "pretending" with a parent or sibling. Humans, perhaps analogously, enter into the make believe play of a motion picture, observe the consequences of certain behavior, and share the emotions of certain characters in the film, without being exposed to the same extent or in the same way to the physical and/or psychological dangers to which the film's characters are exposed. A motion picture makes it possible for viewers, in a purely cognitive space, to test the efficacy of certain strategies and feel the exhilaration of victory, the relief of a "close shave," or the devastation of defeat without the risks that would attend that behavior in the real world.

Play as Cognitive Practice

The major objection leveled against the theory of play as practice is that it requires prescience, pre-knowledge on the part of neonates of those skills that would be required of them as adults. Even the introduction into the theory of an instinct for imitation has failed to completely solve the problem, for higher mammals, such as primates, often find themselves in constantly changing circumstances or environments in which the repertoire of behavioral skills that could be acquired from parents or other adults are likely to be inadequate to the circumstances in which individuals find themselves as adults. In other words, it is not safe to assume that the skills that served one generation adequately will, under continually changing circumstances, serve the next generation sufficiently to ensure survival.

It is, however, possible to consider the theory of play as practice in the context of Piaget's assimilation/accommodation model, as Sue Taylor Parker has done. Assimilation and accommodation are processes that for Piaget form the basis of intelligence. Assimilation is the process whereby children interpret, construct, structure or restructure the objects of their attention (objects in the broadest sense, including interactions, observations of situations, and so forth) in accordance with their already existing cognitive structures. Accommodation is the process by which those interpretations, constructs, or structures are modified through interaction with the real world.

Piaget posited four major phases in the development of a child: sensorimotor (birth to two years), pre-operational (two to seven years), concrete operations (seven to twelve years), and formal operations (twelve years to adult). He emphasized that these stages are not discrete in the sense that earlier behaviors are left behind as the succeeding phases take over, but that a process of layering occurs, with earlier behaviors continuing through the individual's lifetime. It is at the second stage, the pre-operational phase (two to seven years) that the child voluntarily enters into the world of make believe. Play, according to Piaget, is characterized by the primacy of assimilation over accommodation. It is an essentially creative activity, which occurs apart from the normal flow of events, free from the consequences of the real situation.

From such an understanding of play, Parker arrives at a convincing argument for play as not only practice of adult skills in a direct sensorimotor way, but as *cognitive* practice, as an activity that develops problem-solving capacity, cognitive and ideational flexibility, skills that are sufficiently open-ended to be equated with the adaptability required by evolutionary processes. "It is no coincidence," she writes, "that we are both the most playful and the most intelligent of animals."[4] Play is, in fact, a phylogenetically later development among mammals and is correlated with larger brain size. And there is little doubt that play occurs more frequently among animals that thrive in changing conditions, conditions that would require the most flexibility on the part of the organism. "The very animals that play most are those animals which exhibit variable and adaptive behavior as adults and tend to inhabit environmental niches where conditions are not fixed."[5]

This learning or acquisition of skills is a by-product of the play behavior, not the motivation for it. Although the behavioral and cognitive adaptability or flexibility that play fosters in the individual members of a species may be the evolutionary reason for its existence, it should not be confused with the incipient causes of the behavior in any given individual. This point cannot be overemphasized—play is an activity entered into voluntarily for enjoyment. The fact that it is also instructive allows individuals to better cope with their world. It renders them more "fit" for survival. Evolution in this way validates the choice (to play) made by the individual; it selects for it.

The Desire to Play

We humans find ourselves with not only the capacity to play, but an active disposition to play. Both the capacity and the disposition to play are genetically endowed, but why do we *want* to play? What is the motivation for such activity?

An intriguing proposal is that human activity is an effort to maintain optimal (not maximal, but optimal) arousal. Arousal, in this model, refers to generalized arousal of the organism, which results from output from the Reticulate Arousal System:

> The evidence clearly implicates the reticulate arousal system as the mediating mechanism responsible for the process of arousal. The RAS is a diffuse network in the lower brain contiguous with both the afferent pathway carrying sensory input from the body and outside to the cortex and the efferent pathways descending from the brain to the peripheral nervous system. It receives collateral fibres from the sensory tracts and provides indirect routes to the higher brain for incoming stimulation by means of multitudinous connections with the cerebral cortex. The cortex and the reticulate arousal system (RAS) are intimately connected and stand on opposite sides of a balance, with the RAS exerting an arousing influence on the body system generally and the cortex inhibiting the RAS. The resultant effect determines the level of arousal of the animal.[6]

Increasing the level of arousal increases performance to a point, up to some optimal level, after which performance falls off (inverted U function), and humans will typically attempt to act to change the level of arousal to maintain an optimal level: they will doodle or hum when they are bored (understimulated), and they will "escape" from a situation of overstimulation or attend only to parts of the incoming stimulation if they find themselves in a situation from which they cannot escape.

Assuming, then, that human beings seek to maintain optimal arousal, the question immediately arises as to which kinds of stimuli will produce the desired effect. If one contrasts the notion of *optimal* arousal to that of maximal arousal it becomes apparent that under the optimal paradigm the stimulation one seeks, the stimulation that provides the most satisfaction, is new but not too new. The stimulation must be something that can connect to existing schemata but will modify them only slightly, stretching them a little bit—not something so totally novel as to have no associations, no sense of familiarity in any way whatsoever, with nothing to relate to or connect to in our attempts to assimilate the new information. "Intermediate novelty seems to be preferred. Complete or absolute novelty poses problems in that there are no extant categories against which the new experience can be compared. The absolutely novel experience presumably carries an aversively high arousal potential."[7]

Some of the most revealing studies that lead to an arousal-level theory of motivation were done in the area of sensory deprivation. Subjects were deprived of stimulation in a variety of ways and the effects noted. For instance, in one study subjects were "suspended weightless in turbulance-free water at skin temperature in a soundproof tank and told to hang passively. The early reports were alarming. Although the self-reports showed that after an initial sleep the experience was aversive, several subjects maintained their deprivation until they hallucinated. Afterwards their behavior was disturbed in a variety of ways, sometimes for several weeks."[8] For our purposes it is not so much the effects of stimulus deprivation but the kinds of stimuli required to eliminate the aversive effects that is of interest. Not just any stimulation would do:

> The crucial factor seemed to be presence of meaningful patterns in the stimuli. A hissing or white noise may generate the same quantum of energy in the ears, but the subject cannot generate from it patterns of input that can be attended to. The elimination of form, pattern, or meaning from the input to the subject results in perpetual deprivation, as distinguished from the elimination of all stimuli or sensory deprivation.[9]

There is, then, a need for meaning, for information, for pattern and form in the stimulus in order to maintain optimal arousal. It is presumably this kind of stimulation or novelty the human animal seeks. This is the active viewer, the purposive, meaning-seeking individual who views a motion picture. As Gombrich has many times reminded us, the "effort after meaning" begins the moment we open our eyes.[10]

The model of an active, meaning-seeking, human mind is a dynamic one when seen in the context of maintaining optimal arousal. It is a model that contains great flexibility, the stimuli able to provide that optimal level of arousal differing from one situation to another and one individual to another depending upon the set or expectations of the individual, existing cognitive schemata, even the current level of fatigue, just to mention a few of the factors involved.

One group of investigators coined the term *pacers* to describe optimally arousing stimuli. They explain: "Some stimuli may be too complex to act as pacers. A person just learning French will not improve on being exposed to Proust or Beaudelaire, though he may be able to evaluate their work as much more complex than that in his elementary text."[11]

Clearly, there is an ever increasing complexity desired by individuals in their interaction with their environment. As they develop new, broader, and more complex schemata, and as they learn to obtain higher order information from the optic array, they will be able to assimilate and will seek more complex and challenging situations. Their own complexity and flexibility increases, rendering them better able to cope with new or unexpected events.

Consider in this context the educated or experienced film viewer who is better able to assimilate novel or unexpected filmic techniques and perhaps becomes more demanding in that regard. Such a viewer may become bored by the styles and conventions of mainstream narrative films and prefer the challenge of less conventional techniques in so-called art house or experimental films. Those films, on the other hand, might be inaccessible and therefore boring to the less experienced viewer. Viewers seek pacers appropriate for them, for their level of film experience (the complexity of their cognitive schemata), and for their mental state at the time. ("I'm not in the mood for a heavy film tonight.")

Unlike the professional chess player of Neisser's example, who can never go back to playing the game or seeing the chessboard as an amateur does, a professional film viewer *can* see a traditional narrative film in much the same way an amateur film viewer does. One's absorption in the narrative and the diegesis occurs in such films at a largely perceptual level, and we are all professional perceivers.

The Capacity to Frame

Though it has been a difficult task for psychologists to clearly define play, it is one of those elements of behavior that most people agree is readily recognizable. It is relatively easy to get consensus from all observers of a given behavioral situation as to whether it is or is not play. The ease of identification is due in part to the existence of what have been called *play signals* or play frames—precisely the kind of behavior our family dog Sophie exhibited in initiating play activity. Paul Martin presents a straightforward introduction to play signals: "Most mammals have identifiable visual, auditory, tactile or olfactory signals that serve to initiate or maintain social play or to denote that 'what follows is play.' These play signals are sometimes the only motor patterns that are specific to play."[12] He observes that in kittens "certain motor patterns, such as the half-crouch and pounce, are frequently used to initiate social play bouts."[13] Sue Taylor Parker adds to the list of species-specific play signals: "The dog's wagging tail, extended forepaws and cocked head; the monkey's bouncing gait and relaxed open mouthed face; the child's bouncing and laughter, are all examples of such signals. . . . These and other signals, such as bouncing, tagging and running off with a backward glance, often serve as invitations to another animal."[14]

For human behavior, it is instructive not only to think of play signals that initiate or invite play behavior, but also to consider the whole of play activity as a framed event, marked and set apart from other kinds of activity, as an activity having its own kind of rules, its own time and space, its own universe—a world that exists within but apart from that other outer world where the contingencies of reality impinge. In an incisive and insightful essay, Gregory Bateson uses analogies to the picture frame and to mathematical set theory to illustrate the concept of such a psychological frame:

> Psychological frames are related to what we have called "premises." The picture frame tells the viewer that he is not to use the same sort of thinking in interpreting the picture that he might use in interpreting the wallpaper outside the frame. Or, in terms of the analogy from set theory, the messages enclosed within the imaginary line are defined as members of a class by virtue of their sharing common premises or mutual relevance. The frame itself thus becomes a part of the premise system. Either, as in the case of the play frame, the frame is involved in the evaluation of the messages it contains, or the frame merely assists the mind in understanding the contained messages by reminding the thinker that these messages are mutually relevant and the messages outside the frame may be ignored.[15]

The play signal, then, functions as a metacommunicative message, a message not about the content of the play, but the nature or status of the activity.

Participants in play must know that "this is play." Such a metacommunicative message must both initiate the activity and in some way be repeated throughout the course of the activity, lest the critical distinction between play and non-play break down. It is this need for continual reminders of the nature or status of the activity to which Brian Sutton-Smith and Diana Kelly-Byrne refer when they assert that "in play the metacommunicative function always retains primacy. It is apparently essential to keep in the minds of the players that they are indeed playing. . . . To this end, play requires a display of sufficient cues to keep the distinction between this realm and others in the forefront of awareness."[16]

If the activity of movie viewing is to be seen as a type of play, then how is the activity framed or set apart from other reality? How is the invitation "Let's pretend" issued, and how is the primacy of metacommunication maintained?

The usual moviegoing experience is overtly, even verbally framed. We have a word for the object of our attention that separates it categorically: movie. And we go to a place specifically designated for that activity: the movie theater (or our den or living room perhaps to watch a video tape). Furthermore, the film/video is itself circumscribed, framed by the theater or video screen (the "frame" as it is sometimes called). Finally, within a given film or video, the "pretending" is framed by opening titles and closing credits. The entire event is thus set apart by multiple frames and thereby distinguished from other realms of reality.

Although the event is already set apart from other reality, it might well be argued that the invitation "Let's pretend," the personal invitation to the individual viewer to voluntarily enter into the diegetic world and actively participate in the pretend play, is not specifically issued until the opening of the film. It is often issued in the traditional narrative by that opening sequence of shots that all of us recognize: the long shot of a crowd as the camera moves in closer and closer, finally to settle upon one figure or one face in the crowd; or the movement from shot of city to shot of building to shot of window in that building, to the action taking place inside the room with the window. The movement inward, often the familiar structure of LS-MS-CU, draws viewers into the diegesis, introduces them to the characters, and involves them in the action.

Similar signals or frames are necessary within a film/video narrative to introduce any shift from one realm to another:

into (or out of) flashbacks or flash forwards, imaginary or fantasy sequences, dreams or hallucinations. Many such devices have been used precisely for the purpose of marking the change in level: blurred focus, gauze or filters over the camera lens, shifts from black-and-white to color or vice versa, iris shots, and a variety of mattes. Failure to supply adequate signals for a change in the image's status (for example, into or out of flashback, dream, or fantasy) results in viewer confusion. Even when part of the filmic style, as for example in Alain Resnais' *Last Year at Marienbad*, if the viewer is either unable or unwilling to supply the transitional signals himself, the result is at least temporary bewilderment if not aversive incomprehension.

The way in which motion pictures maintain the frame is particularly interesting. It is one of the highly consequential by-products of the nature of visual representation. The primacy of metacommunciation, the continual reinforcement of the message "This is pretend," is maintained on the *perceptual* level, through the push-pull, in and out of the illusion of reality that (as discussed earlier) results from the essential ambiguity of the visual image. That alternation between immersion in the illusion of reality and awareness of the illusion as illusion asserts both the difference in status of the diegetic world and its coexistence with external reality, thereby maintaining the frame.

Because that periodic foregrounding of the metacommunicative message "This is pretend" or "This is a movie" is achieved on the perceptual level, and because there is such an overt framing of the film viewing event (on a screen in a theater, and so forth) an intra-filmic device for asserting "This is a movie" is rendered unnecessary. And in practice, any such attempt to access reality by "revealing the work" comes up against what I have come to call *Branigan's Paradox*. Edward Branigan's argument is that even if you break the diegesis, you do not thereby gain a glimpse of reality.[17] You simply create another formal element in the narrative (of lights, cameras, cables, and microphones) or another embedded "world" within the film. It is all occurring inside the framed event, which we already know is of a different order than the reality outside the frame.

The diegesis might as well remain unbroken. The viewer need not be protected from "absorption." It is not necessary to "reveal the work" of a motion picture; we can *see* that "this is pretend." And a seamless fictional world is a source of tremendous power in the cinema—it provides a stable and continuous basis for the involvement of the viewer in the experience of the film. The viewer can maintain an uninterrupted emotional/psychological involvement in the diegesis, allowing the impact of the film to build to maximum effect.

It is instructive to contemplate how the viewing experience would be changed if somehow it were possible for the film-as-play itself to be unframed, indistinguishable from reality. Consider the implications of the "myth of total cinema," which André Bazin tells us constitutes the origins of cinema.[18] Referring to the "precursors of the cinema," Bazin writes: "In their imagination they saw the cinema as a total and complete representation of reality; they saw in a trice the reconstruction of a perfect illusion of the outside world in sound, color and relief."[19] Such a "perfect illusion" might provide the ultimate pleasure, but if the circumstances of viewing and the boundaries of the illusion itself were not explicitly framed, the effect could be profoundly disturbing.

Perhaps the closest analog in our media-rich environment is the deep psychological discomfort instilled in the viewing public by the reenactment of news items. In unmarked news reenactments we have an instance of failure to give proper metacommunicative signals as to the nature of the image. Is it factual or fictional? The lack of distinction is the source of much discomfort and the focus of considerable controversy.

Perhaps the discomfort arises from the fact that the framing of the play event, the separating of one realm of reality from another, is not optional. Framing is dictated by the nature of cognitive processing, by the functioning of the mind itself.

The ability to clearly discriminate reality from fantasy and external stimulation originating in the physical world from the internal stimulation of one's own stream of consciousness is necessary for functional behavior and ultimately for sanity. It is precisely the inability to manipulate frames and to correctly interpret metacommunicative signals that Bateson identifies as the basic problem of the neurotic and the schizophrenic.

The fundamental nature of this need for discrimination of reality from fantasy, as well as its innate biological (rather than cultural) character is demonstrated by Kohlberg's cross-cultural study in "a society where adults genuinely believe that dreams are manifestations of reality and must be viewed as externally derived messages." Kohlberg reports: "The children first go through a phase of learning quite on their own that dreams are inner manifestations and then once having reached this point at about age 12, they begin to adopt the adult-influenced cultural stereotype."[20] The lesson is that fantasy can inform our perception of reality, but fundamentally nature has equipped us to perceive veridical information and to set our fantasies apart so that we can be sure that we are acting upon the former rather than the latter. To perceive something directly is to believe. On the other hand, to believe something to be reality that is by nature a framed activity involves a leap of the mind, requiring the support of tradition and the assistance of intellectual effort, or perhaps disease.

Summary

Movies are, of course, seen not only by children but also by adults. The question inevitably arises as to whether one continues to play into adulthood. What we normally regard as play activity is usually observed in children and gradually diminishes with age.

The critical term here is *observed*: the play of children is physical and observable, while the "play" of the adult mind usually is not. Michael Ellis in *Why People Play* notes:

> The confusing element is merely that the stimulus-seeking behavior of adult humans may not result in any overt behavior since the interplay of stimulus events can be entirely cognitive, whereas in the young interactions are more often between cognitive events and physical events. As the properties of the immediate environment become known, the adult human retreats into his brain or indulges in more sophisticated explorations of the environment not normally classified as play.[21]

The viewing of a motion picture might well be considered one such exploration of the environment, an instance of the adult human mind at play.

A motion picture is a framed event, and we enter into its space and time by stepping through the frame, by playing "Let's pretend." Watching a movie is not *like* play and it is not a metaphor for play; it *is* play.

As with any form of play, it is engaged in for pleasure, but it also can contribute to our growth and development. The same could be said, of course, for reading a book. But the motion picture has an even more fundamental avenue of accessibility. It presents to the visual system an optical array and to the auditory system a pattern of molecular disturbance that, for lack of an alternative, is processed as is information from the natural world. In doing so, perception itself confers upon the fictional world of the film the status of a world that can be seen with one's eyes and heard with one's ears.

8
Character

To recognize another person as a distinct individual, to be able to read his emotions, to intuit his intentions, has always been crucial to our survival. In the distant past, our lives depended upon our ability to accurately recognize and judge the moral character of other individuals of our own species. It is no less the case today; we must quickly judge whether we can trust a new acquaintance; we must know whether he will befriend or exploit us. Likewise, we must be able to quickly recognize old acquaintances, and we must continually update our assessments of their characters. The problems of character recognition and attribution are universal. The capacities to cope with these problems were developed through evolution, and the manifestations of those capacities are, as we might expect, similar from culture to culture.

It should not surprise us that a major artifact from our own culture deals with the issue of character. The artifact, a motion picture from 1941, Orson Welles' *Citizen Kane*, is generally considered to be one of the most important, perhaps *the* most important, motion picture ever made. Perhaps it is more than coincidence that we attribute such importance to a movie that deals with a human problem so central to our survival, that of character attribution. In both form and content *Citizen Kane* is an exploration of character, of a man's character, an exploration of those attributes that make him different from all other human beings, an exploration of those attributes that make him better or worse than other human beings.

Security fences dissolve into wrought iron gates that enclose a fantasy land of monkeys in a cage, gondolas in a misty lagoon, and reconstructions of classical ruins. A castle dominates this bizarre landscape, and high in its upthrust towers a lighted window goes dark. From inside that same window the first light of dawn appears, the brightness from outside the window revealing a figure stretched out upon a bed and covered up to his waist with a sheet and blanket. In his hand he holds an object that reflects the morning light. Snowflakes fill the screen, and the falling flakes slowly dissolve to a close-up view of a miniature cabin with snow piled high upon its roof. The shot rapidly widens to reveal the glass ball that contains the miniature cabin and the hand that holds the ball. The snowflakes continue falling as the picture cuts to an extreme close-up of a mustached mouth that utters one word: "Rosebud."

Cut to the hand that loses its grip upon the snow covered cabin and its miniature world inside the glass. The ball falls from the hand and rolls down a couple of steps. A cut to the reverse angle, and we see the ball fall from the last step and shatter upon the floor, splashing its contents audibly onto the lens of the camera and into our faces.

Distorted as though through the curved broken glass we see the door to the room open and a nurse enter. Cut to a view near the cabin toppled upon its side looking through the debris of the shattered miniature world, and the nurse crosses the room to the bed. Cut to the nurse folding the hand that held the ball along with the other hand in the crossed chest self-embrace of death. She pulls the sheet slowly over his hands and face. We return to the long shot of the bed before the window, but now the crystalline globe is gone, and the body is completely covered with the sheet.

Who is this man who lived in such a strange and fanciful place, whose death we witnessed, whose last utterance is burned into our memories? We want to know. And, of course, the remainder of the movie is constructed around the answering of this question. Who was Charles Foster Kane? What kind of a man was he? We have witnessed his departure from the world. This is his judgment day, and we the audience are his judges.

A movie such as *Citizen Kane* is a very complex construction, an intricate, precisely sequenced program designed to interface with human visual and auditory systems, and having gained access in this way, to "run" in the mind of a viewer. And it does "run." We do see and hear, experience emotions, understand causes and consequences, and remember what we have known. We are one with Thompson, who concludes, "You know, all the same, I feel kind of sorry for Mr. Kane," and with Susan, who replies, "Don't you think I do?" But we engage with the movie, even at this level, automatically, without effort on our part, and we would have not the slightest notion of how it all comes about if it were not for researchers laboring for the smallest of gains, reveling in the tiniest insight into how the mind actually works.

Recognition

How do we recognize other individuals? How do we come to know their moral character? Why do we see the disembodied image of an actor as a fictional character in a fictional world? Why do we attribute moral character to these phantoms on the screen? These are fascinating questions, and the answers to them are at present sketchy and incomplete. Will future researchers answer them more fully? Will film scholars be among those in the forefront of the search? I think so. Much work has been done already.

Where do we begin in our effort to answer the first of these questions concerning how we recognize and identify other individuals? We might start by asking how early in our lives we begin the process of recognition. We are already suspicious of the notion that infants are born with a tabula rasa. We suspect that they may come into this world with some programs or schemata already in place.

A particular schemata or set of expectations allows one to pick up one set of information rather than another. The environment is overdetermined—more information is available than one could ever process. An individual's schemata will

determine which set is salient to him, which set he will perceive. Perception is probably selective rather than constructive.
As Neisser put it: "Perceptual schemata disambiguate by *selecting* a particular alternative, not by adding more evidence
for it."[1] He has also suggested that there is never a time when
we are altogether without such schemata. "The newborn infant opens his eyes onto a world that is infinitely rich in
information: he has to be ready for some of it if he is to engage
in the perceptual cycle and become ready for more.... What
babies ... know, I believe, is how to find out about their environment, and how to organize the information they obtain
so it can help them obtain more. They do not know even this
very well, but well enough to begin."[2]

Infants consistently exhibit such information-gathering activity as looking toward sounds, following objects with their
eyes, and reaching out toward things they see. They choose
to look at novel rather than familiar objects, they prefer moving objects to stationary ones and noisy objects to silent ones.
In short, they prefer situations containing more, rather than
less, information. These are information-seeking creatures.

In a landmark series of experiments carried out by R. L.
Fantz and cited by Eleanor Gibson in *Principles of Perceptual
Learning and Development*, the experimenters placed infants
in a looking chamber on their backs and presented stimuli
to them. They then observed the babies' reactions through a
small peephole. In one experiment, the infants were presented
with three patterned circles (a schematic face, a patch of news-
paper, and a black and white bull's eye) and three plain circles
colored red, white, and yellow. Infants spent much more time
looking at the patterned circles than the plain ones and greatly
preferred the schematic face.

Though Eleanor Gibson correctly observes that we cannot
conclude solely from these experiments that there is instinc-
tive recognition of the human face, she notes that "it is of
evolutionary significance that a face-like pattern appears to
have stimulus characteristics (as yet to be defined) that attract
attention at a very early age."[3] Gibson draws the general con-

clusion that "primates have few innate specific responses to specific stimuli, but have, rather, an innate capacity for selective visual exploration."[4] Here Eleanor Gibson is in accord with Ulric Neisser who suggests that in infants there are basic and very adaptable schemata that engage the environment and are modified by it in an ongoing series of perceptual cycles. One of these is an interest in the human face. Other innate schemata seem to have been developed in the same ways by all human beings and exist in similar form in *adults* cross-culturally. Some of these universal schemata facilitate recognition of other people and by extension to recognition of characters encountered on a movie screen.

James Cutting and Dennis Proffitt started their research in an effort to test the notion that people can recognize other individuals by their gait, by the way they walk. The experimenters first took six people who knew each other and taped spots of fluorescent tape at each of their joints (ankle, knee, hip, shoulder, and so forth). They then videotaped each of them walking, adjusting the video so that only the spots of light from the reflective tape were visible. And indeed, the subjects could recognize their friends by their walk.

At this point, the experiment took an interesting turn. Cutting and Proffitt decided to use a paradigm that has been eloquently described by David Marr. Such a paradigm consists of a computational theory (about what is being processed and why), an algorithm (a computational procedure), and hardware implementation (physical implementation of the computation).[5] First they showed the videotapes of people walking (with only the spots of light at their joints visible) to observers who did not know the walkers. The result was that even people who did not know the walkers could nevertheless distinguish between male and female walkers. On the basis of such findings, Cutting and Proffitt proposed that the motion alone (as conveyed by the points of light) contained information about gender.

In keeping with the paradigm, they then devised an algorithm that was a computation of the center of motion for each figure. (This may or may not be the algorithm the human mind uses, but in this way they demonstrated that a computation is possible.) From such computations they were able to synthesize the motion on a computer, that is, create a set of points of light that satisfied the algorithm. When they showed the computer simulations based upon the algorithm to experimental subjects, the subjects were in agreement as to the gender of the walkers represented by the dots on the video screen.

In an unrelated but strikingly similar experiment, John Bassili studied the recognition of emotion by covering the faces of actors with black greasepaint spotted with white dots. He then asked them to convey various emotions and videorecorded them in such a way that only the white dots were visible on the screen. When the videotapes were shown to experimental subjects, the viewers were generally able to recognize that a face was expressing an emotion, and to identify the specific emotion, from the slight movement of the dots on the screen.

Taken together, these studies lend support to a computational theory of perception, for algorithms could presumably be found for the movement of the dots in the experiment dealing with the recognition of facial expression of emotion, just as an algorithm was found for the movement of the dots representing gender difference in walking. The implications of these experiments for motion picture theory are also significant. If people watching a video screen presentation can recognize gender in the one case and emotion from a few white dots moving on a screen in the other, then surely the information in motion pictures is overdetermined. Apparently there is great redundancy. The process of perceiving a motion picture must be one of *selecting* information as Neisser suggests, not one of constructing something from impoverished stimuli. And one of the things we somehow know to select for when faced with the task of identifying a person or judging his emotion is the information contained in body motion and facial motion.

A number of studies have also been carried out that measured the ability to judge what a person is feeling, the ability
to read his emotions. Usually in such studies, an actor displays an emotion and subjects are asked to judge what emotion
the actor has displayed. The studies have sometimes been
criticized for using actors, and some researchers have attempted to photograph real people having real emotions, but
it comes as no surprise to those of us who have studied film
that the results are pretty much the same. If this were not the
case, the whole enterprise of dramatic narrative film, not to
mention theater, would be impossible. It makes little difference whether the emotions are presented by a competent actor
or are real. We judge a person's internal emotion by outward
appearances, and we do that both in real life and in viewing
a film or photograph or videotape.

From the experiment by Bassili in which observers correctly
judged emotion from a display of phosphorescent dots painted
on the face of an actor, one might suppose that the capacity
to read the emotions of another person is a universal human
characteristic, a capacity that is either inherent or easily acquired. But do we all read the emotions the same way? Are
there individual or cultural differences in the perception of
emotion? Ekman and Friesen report several experiments dealing with the cross-cultural perception of emotion. They found
some persuasive universals and a few interesting exceptions.

In one study, Americans were asked to identify the emotions expressed by members of a visually isolated New Guinea
culture.[6] The Americans were able to distinguish anger, disgust, happiness, and sadness from each other and from fear
and surprise, but the American observers could not distinguish the New Guinea portrayals of fear and surprise.[7] In
another experiment reported in the same study, photos of facial expressions were shown to subjects in twelve different
literate cultures, and they were generally able to identify the
emotions expressed.

It is critical in this context to take care not to confuse the
expression of emotion (which seems to be directly available

and biologically based) with the display of emotion (which is largely controlled by cultural conventions). Even though facial expressions and the understanding of them appears to be universal, there may be culturally specific display rules. That is, the circumstances under which it is appropriate to display certain emotions may vary from culture to culture. For example, in another experiment reported by Ekman and Friesen, Friesen (in a 1972 experiment) showed films to American and Japanese subjects and with a hidden camera recorded facial expressions. The expressions captured by the hidden camera were very similar in the two cultures. However, when an experimenter was present with the subjects, "the Japanese more than the Americans masked negative expressions with smiles."[8]

Attribution

In a film, of course, we see not only faces and expressions of emotion but entire events and sequences of events. We see behavior. And on the basis of that behavior we attribute character or disposition. When we know what is predictable and stable in our interaction with the environment, that is, when we can perceive the invariants in our world, we can then deal with the unpredictable and unstable elements. In matters of person perception, *character* or disposition constitutes that invariant.

Edward Jones and Keith Davis carried out research in social psychology in the mid-sixties that laid the groundwork of what has come to be known as attribution theory. They, like Fritz Heider before them, were interested in commonsense psychology, the kinds of rules of thumb or shortcuts we use to sort out our everyday perceptions. When it comes to looking at a person's actions and attributing character to that person (he must be such-and-such kind of person to have behaved in that way) we all use the same kind of short-cut approach. "The perceiver seeks to find *sufficient reason* why the person acted and why the act took on a particular form."[9] That is to say, we do not look for an ultimate reason or a long chain of causes and effects that led to a particular action. Instead, we seek a sufficient reason for a person's actions and make a judgment of the person's character on that basis. We settle for the first plausible explanation for the behavior that has been observed.

Jones and Davis propose a model whereby one observes an action and one or more effects. On the basis of that observation, we make a judgment about a person's character. This relationship Jones and Davis called "correspondence." The model, they say, "systematically accounts for a perceiver's inferences about what an actor was trying to achieve."[10] Based upon the observer's estimate of the actor's intentions, he judges the actor's disposition or character. In doing so, Jones and Davis maintain, observers follow a kind of psychological rule of thumb which they describe as an expression of Heider's general balance principle.[11] "Bad actions come from bad people, and good is achieved by the good."[12]

Note the primacy of intention here, which is functional in an evolutionary sense and is of the greatest significance in relation to the comprehension of narrative film. As observers, we are compelled to attribute character based upon the actions and behavior we observe, and we apparently make the assumptions Jones and Davis have identified in arriving at the first available explanation of why a person behaved in a particular way. The analogy to judging characters in film is direct: the first time we see a character, he behaves in a certain way, and based upon that behavior, we categorize the character.

Perhaps the category most readily available (the sufficient reason or first plausible explanation to which Jones and Davis refer) is a prototype or stereotype (such as the bored suburban housewife, the whore with a heart of gold, the ruthless businessman). And indeed, we often proceed this way in judging the characters in a motion picture: first we categorize the character by prototype and then we modify that hypothesis as the action unfolds, observing how much divergence there is from the prototype. The greater the ultimate modification the more "complex" the character. In the case where no modification of the initial prototype occurs, we speak of a "flat" or "cardboard" character.

The initial categorization of the character, however impulsive and however accurate or inaccurate, serves a purpose for film viewers. It provides them with a set of expectations that can be modified as necessary in the course of viewing the film. Those expectations provide a substantial part of the raw material for the momentum and comprehensibility of a narrative film.

But let us return to a question raised earlier. We observed that actors were frequently used in experimental work done on cross-cultural emotion recognition, and that it seemed to make little difference whether the emotion was feigned or real. It is true that we judge internal emotional states by outward appearances and that this fact makes acting as we know it possible. But is this the only reason that we are willing to accept an actor as a character on the screen in a narrative film? In chapter 7, we discussed the intricate connection between the human mind's capacity for pretend or symbolic play and the ability to enter the diegesis, the fictional world of a film. I would suggest that the film viewer's capacity to accept an actor playing the part of a character is also connected to that capacity for play, for role taking and role assignment are a central part of the symbolic play observed in childhood. Furthermore, the same dual awareness of framed event and reality that characterizes the diegetic involvement, and indeed the very act of viewing a motion picture, is present in the actor/character perception of a film viewer. We know alternately (and ultimately simultaneously) that the person we see on the screen is both Orson Welles and Charles Foster Kane.

It is important to remember in approaching an activity as complex as character attribution that all of this activity springs from mechanisms developed by evolution in order to further our information-gathering capacities, to help us make sense of our world. The perceptual and cognitive activity involved in film viewing is the same activity we human beings engage in when interacting with the world at large. As such, that activity must be viewed from the perspective of our ecological relationship with that world, our active search for meaningful patterns in an overdetermined environment, and our simultaneous perception of possibilities for action (i.e., affordances) in that world.

Identification

In an ecological model of cognition, one based approximately on Gibson's theory of visual perception, meaning (affordances) cannot simply be perceived abstractly in the events of the world or those of the film we are watching. We, as perceivers, are part of the ecological system, and in the world it is the meaning of events in relation to ourselves that we perceive. To put it another way, I perceive not what something *means* but what it means to me. We are programmed through evolution to perceive meaning in that way, as part of our environment.[13] We cannot therefore just perceive meaning per se in the events of a motion picture. We must perceive meanings in relation to someone, to a character in the movie who inhabits the fictional world of the movie, who is subject to its constraints and affordances.

We usually think of the protagonist of a narrative, whether in a book, on the stage, or in a videotape or a movie, as the person the story is about, the main character of the story. It is an intriguing possibility to consider that privileged character as the one we choose to use as our reference for the interpretation of meaning. We see the events of the fictional world through this person's eyes, as it were. Not that we see only what that character sees or are restricted to what that character knows and feels, but that it is *his* fate, *his* survival or well-being or comfort that we care about, just as it is our own survival or well-being that is our ultimate concern as we make our way in our world.

I have proposed an ecological approach to character identification. But how would such an approach apply to our viewing of *Citizen Kane*? The movie is constructed so that we the viewers must sit in judgment of Kane's character. But a profound indecision engulfs us, and a potentially hazardous hesitation afflicts us. Our own character, our own souls are in grave danger, for as members of the audience we must not only render an intellectual judgment as to the moral fitness of the subject on trial, we must at a most primitive emotional level, decide to identify or not identify with the character Charles Foster Kane. We might choose instead to identify with the reporter, Thompson, who has been assigned to solve the mystery of Rosebud, and in the process the mystery of Kane's character. But he is purposely ill-defined, and we seldom see his face. He remains a shadowy player in a story that is clearly about Kane. Or perhaps we could identify with one of the other narrators; there are five of them, but not one offers a continuing basis for our identification. There is only Kane himself, and to identify with him we run a moral risk. We perhaps identify at first, but then pull back. We totter upon the threshold of our own moral irresolution as we witness Kane, in flashback, living his.

A simple notion of identification with a protagonist or single character does not appear to be adequate. Perhaps the generalized concept of identification needs to be broken down into at least three specific components: *perspective-taking, caring*, and what I will call *role identification*.

To evaluate the affordances in a narrative context (that is, in a diegetic world), one must perceive them in relationship to a character in that world; one must, in other words, perceive them from that character's perspective. The protagonist usually has a problem to solve or a goal to achieve. Whether we are able to share the protagonist's definition of the problem or understand his motivation for pursuing a particular goal, that is, share his perspective, is a factor in our experience of the movie. We may comprehend quite clearly how the protagonist sees things and either disagree or even actively oppose his view, or we may simply fail to care whether he solves his problem, overcomes the obstacles, or achieves his goal.

Not caring results in a disinterest on the part of the viewer, in a lack of sympathy for the protagonist, and in a failure of involvement. A lack of caring concerning the fortunes of the protagonist is quite a different phenomenon from the "malicious joy" (to use Heider's term) that one may experience at the misfortune of the antagonist. Such joy is itself a form of caring and constitutes a major affordance of film viewing. Not caring, in the sense of the present definition, is of the sort that might result in a level of boredom prompting the viewer to switch channels if watching the movie on television. If, as a viewer, one can comprehend the perspective of the protagonist and care whether he achieves his goals, then one will probably not switch channels; one will likely get caught up in the narrative and stick with the movie to the end to see how it comes out. The reference to plot is obvious, but it can be argued that the essential satisfaction one seeks in regard to character is afforded in seeing the protagonist achieve his goal, and in perhaps equal measure seeing the antagonist get his comeuppance.

There is yet another satisfaction associated with a fictional character that is not necessary to one's enjoyment of a film but is a sort of bonus if available, and it will be available to some members of an audience and not others. Such satisfaction is related to our capacity to play, to pretend, and is manifest in role identification. At ten years old it is easy for children to view a movie and pretend that they are the hero, that is, to actively take on the role of the protagonist (even though they know that they is not in fact that person). For adults, such imaginative pretending may not come so easily, but the capacity for all play is not lost, and adults may identify something of themselves in the protagonist. Movies are, after all, a form of adult play, and the marshalling of what one perceives to be his own character traits against overwhelming obstacles and perhaps achieving confirmation of their virtue and effectiveness, can be pleasurable and self-affirming. What I have been describing are goods that a movie might afford the viewer first hand. From moment to moment, however, meanings for the viewer are secondhand, presented as affordances for the characters in relation to their fictional world.

In *Citizen Kane*, we perceive affordances from Thompson's perspective: his task is to solve the puzzle of Kane's character, and in taking his perspective, we ask ourselves the following: What does this or that information tell us about Charles Foster Kane? What does it add to our understanding of the man? Is there a clue here as to who or what Rosebud is? Thompson, however, is not the protagonist we *care* about. The film/script/program is carefully designed to prevent our caring about the person of Thompson. We hardly know him as a character. He is a shadowy presence (but a necessary presence, for we need a character whose perspective we can adopt). It does, however, ensure that what we do care about, along with Thompson, is his quest to better understand the man whose dying word was *Rosebud*. We become as obsessed with that search as Thompson himself, and finally the quest takes on a life of its own and outlives even Thompson's presence; we alone as viewers are given the final piece of the puzzle.

Thompson stands in the hallway with a group of other reporters. He is attempting to answer their questions when Katherine, who must have just returned from an assignment in outer Mongolia, asks, "What's Rosebud?" Cut to a shot of Thompson in the foreground facing the group; the camera pulls back on Raymond's line, "That's what he said when he died," and pauses for a moment as Thompson tosses the piece of a puzzle he holds in his hand into the box held by Katherine. The camera resumes its pullback as Thompson takes the box from her, turns, and moving into the foreground, places the box upon a table. The discussion continues and Thompson, admitting defeat in his search for Rosebud, turns back to the group, but the camera, now guided by the hand of an unseen storyteller, continues its retreat all the way to the rafters. From our high perch, we see Thompson put on his coat and lead the others away to catch their train. Dissolve to an even higher vantage point as the reporters make their way between the crates to their exit. Dissolve to a quiet clutter of crates way below. Dissolve and begin a steady and purposeful glide over the tops of the hundreds of crates and downward, veering only slightly to the right, to frame a sled nestled among what appear to be Mary Kane's household effects. Two hands reach in from out of frame and take the sled away. Cut to a longshot of workmen throwing "junk" through the fiery doorway of a furnace. A workman carrying the sled enters the frame and makes straightway for the furnace. The camera follows him to the blazing doorway and rests upon the threshold as he tosses the sled into the flames. Cut to a close-up of the sled in the fire. The varnish bubbles on the surface of the superheated wood and, quickly evaporating, clearly reveals the stencilled white letters R-O-S-E-B-U-D and the rosebud decal beneath. The camera moves in closer to see both the word and the picture consumed in flames. Cut to the exterior with dense smoke rising from the chimney as the sled literally goes up in smoke.

Throughout the film, we have been repeatedly thwarted in our attempts to care about a person. We are held at a distance from Kane. His story is told, not in a continuous chronological narrative, but in bits and pieces, and not just from the perspective of the reporter Thompson, but from his perspective of the stories being told by five different narrators whose own experiences with Kane color their tales, and not infrequently from still another perspective within those tales, that of the implied author of the image we see (by choice of angles, music, lighting, and so forth).[14] We are prevented by the multiplicity of narrative voices from getting close to Kane. Moreover, in many of the incidents described by the film's five diegetic narrators (Thatcher, Leland, Bernstein, Alexander, and Raymond) Kane comes across as a not so likable character. The result is an emotional roller coaster. We are drawn to Kane in one scene, repelled by him in the next; we begin to care but then pull back. All of this reminds us that we are still uncertain of the man. We do not know Charles Foster Kane. We have no firm fix on his character. Our emotional response as viewers is thwarted, but we keep trying. Somehow we want to care, and sometimes we come close (as when we, along with Thompson and Susan, feel sorry for Kane) but the real emotional impact of the film is in this way postponed until the end.

As he is leaving Xanadu having to admit defeat in his efforts to learn the identity of the mysterious "Rosebud," Thompson quips, "I don't think any word can explain a man's life. No, I guess Rosebud is just a piece in a jigsaw puzzle, a missing piece." But as he leaves and the camera pans the crates and boxes he leaves behind, we want to hold him by his coattails and say, "Wait, Rosebud is here somewhere! And it *can* define the man. It will tell us who Charles Foster Kane was, what *he* cared about!" As if in response (to *our* feeling), the camera zooms in on the sled in the furnace and unleashes the emotion that has until this time been thwarted. We now know who Kane was and feel the full tragedy of his life.

In most narrative films, the character whose perspective we take and the character we care about are one in the same, and if in addition to that we also identify with the character (that is, see in his personality something of ourselves) the emotional impact is heightened even more. (In all success-ful characters, of course, there is some element with which we can in some sense identify.) In *Citizen Kane*, however, the emotional impact comes not from identification with the main character, but from the thwarting of that identification, the manipulation of our perspective, the toying with our af-fections, and the postponing of our accepting as our own his search for moral perfection while tripping over his own vanity. Only when we come to know what he cares about, a sled named Rosebud, a cabin in Colorado, and a mother who loved him, can we *identify* with the character of Charlie Kane, see things from his *perspective*, and *care* what happened to him.

Citizen Kane is perhaps the exception that proves the rule.

It is highly unusual for the character with whom one identifies to be someone other than the film's protagonist or for that identification to be deferred until the film's end. But that unusual circumstance in *Citizen Kane* allows us to pull apart and examine the nature of character perception in the motion picture. Because the organizing principle of the film is the quest for the significance of Rosebud, which is Thompson's specific task, we as viewers perceive the affordances of the filmic events through Thompson, asking and finding always partial answers to his question: "Who or what is Rosebud?" As the narrative progresses we, like Thompson, are looking for an answer to that question. What is so unusual (and so intriguing and instructive) about *Citizen Kane* is that only the viewer is provided an answer to that central question, and that critical piece of information allows for the switch to identification with Kane himself. The story becomes not Thompson's quest but Kane's struggle. We go back mentally and reconsider the narrative's events from Kane's point of view in light of the new understanding we have of him. We as film viewers come to feel the tragedy of Kane's life, and we as film theorists come to understand that inside the diegetic envelope of a motion picture things do not just mean, they mean something *to* someone or *for* someone, just as they do inside the ecological envelope of the natural world.

9
Narrative

Stories are familiar to all of us. They are a part of childhood essential to our cognitive development. Stories provide a way to make sense of our own experience and a way to connect with the experience of others. Whether a story is our own or someone else's, the essential principle that guides and defines its construction is that it must convey and at the same time disambiguate experience.

Even the casual observer of child development cannot help but notice that children begin to crawl a few months after birth, and shortly thereafter pull themselves upright, balance precariously on wobbly legs, and walk. Similarly, at about two years of age they say their first words in whatever language those around them are using. Amazingly, children do these things (walk and talk) merely by exposure to the activities of other humans whether or not anyone bothers to teach them. Even more incredibly, as soon as children have attained minimal competence in speaking, they begin narratizing their own experience, as in "Johnny made me cry." And as soon as they are capable of grasping the meaning of a string of verbal utterances, they become fascinated by stories, stories told, stories read to them, stories illustrated in books or presented on a screen. If the tendency to narratize one's own experience and to delight in stories told by others is not innate, then it certainly falls well within the category of those things that are very easily learned, easily learned because the patterns for their eventual realization are there from the beginning in the architecture of the mind, resident in the very connections enabling the physiology of thought itself. Perhaps the capacity for storying resides somewhere in the myriad of neuronal connections that form shortly after birth and then atrophy if unused. Perhaps the schemata for narratizing personal experience and for story appreciation are built upon innate schemata for categorizing driven by the general compulsion to make sense of one's world. Whatever its status may be in the nervous system, narratizing is one of the most powerful mechanisms the human mind possesses for making sense out of the complicated events of the world.

Origins of Narrative

Since we do not know the precise origin of storytelling let us reflect for a moment upon just how primitive the capacity for rudimentary narration might be. Beyond making sense of our experience, is there any practical value in narratizing events? Would it be adaptive for an individual (of any species) to be able to pass on to its successors its experience with the environment? The answer is yes, of course; recipients of such secondhand experience could in this way avoid the dangers and take advantage of the affordances pointed out to them. In fact, the adaptive advantage of a capacity to pass on experience is so apparent that Jean Baptiste de Lamarck assumed it to be a fundamental law of evolution. He achieved enduring notoriety for his error. Darwin proposed, and others have confirmed, that no mechanism exists by which individual experience can be directly encoded into one's genes. Evolution *does*, however, take the experience of individuals into account, but only in a most indirect and indifferent way. For example, an individual bird with a bill that is too small to crack the large shells of nuts constituting the only available food supply, will very likely relinquish its position in the evolutionary chain, while its larger billed cousins survive to pass on their genetically endowed large bills to their offspring. The relationship of individual experience to evolution is that individuals either survive or do not, and the species evolves. How much a species can evolve, that is, the range of its adaption, is related to the diversity of the collective gene pool of survivors.

So if evolution, operating through the basic mechanisms of diversity and natural selection, cannot directly accommodate the transmission of experience from one generation to the next, is it possible for animals not in possession of language to accomplish such a feat at all? Monkeys pass on the experience of grooming, raccoons pass on the experience of food washing, and early humans most likely passed on the experience of hunting and gathering, or perhaps scavenging. But does animal communication contain the rudiments of narration? Consider the wolf who collects the scent of a kill by rolling in the carcass and then takes the scent back to the pack, displays the scent and entices the others to follow him back to the kill. And what about the honeybee who flies away from the hive in search of nectar? It arrives at a peach tree in full bloom at some distance from the hive, collects some sample nectar, and returns to the vicinity of the hive, where it engages the attention of other bees by flying toward them, then turning abruptly, and making a short straight flight, indicating the direction and distance of the peach tree. The honeybee then repeats this act of showing until the other bees are enticed to fly to the source of the nectar themselves. Is the act of the wolf or the honeybee merely animal communication or is it a primitive form of narration? Imagine an upright walking primate (presumably without language) who, having stumbled upon a beehive, returns to his comrades and by gestures and sounds, and perhaps by displaying the stings he has received, conveys his experience with the bees to them. Would this constitute rudimentary narration? The intriguing implication is that the impulse to narratize may be more basic than language itself, that it is the possibility of narrating *experience* that gives language its power.

As the possessors of language, humans are not limited to showing; they can also tell. Humans have the capacity to learn in a way that is unavailable to other animals. They can consciously and willfully ingest information, as do students cramming before an exam. But do not assume that because it is a more recently acquired capacity that this uniquely human method of learning is superior. Animals must learn by experience with their environment, and to do so, even for the human animal, is the phylogenetically older, more fundamental, and probably more compelling way to learn (even if the experience is gained in the framed activity of play).

Personalizing Information

Humans have a clear advantage over other animals when it comes to learning, but as many last minute crammers have discovered, cold, abstract information often has no meaning for the would-be learner and is difficult to retain for long periods of time. An ecological approach sheds a great deal of light upon this common problem. Objects and events are, of course, whatever they are in a physical sense, but meanings are generated in the *relationships* of individuals to such objects and events—the relationships that J. J. Gibson has called affordances. From an ecological point of view, the point of view of an animal walking on the ground, the basic meaning of the event is in its affordance for the individual. For a given event and a given perceiver there may be a large number, although not an infinite number, of possible relationships and therefore meanings.

In narratizing, creating a story, we incorporate the meanings of events. The narration utilizes a chain of causes and effects to lock in or narrow the range of possible meanings. Narratizing allows an individual to stabilize meanings, to learn lessons from his own experience, and to apply this understanding to future situations, thereby gaining a tremendous flexibility, the ability to reformulate past experience in terms of new information or experience. (In this context, it is not surprising that one of the most effective techniques in psychotherapy is to *re-story*, to help the patient rework his experience into a different story.)

Furthermore, since meanings are generated out of an individual's experience with events, meaning can be transmitted in story form by the conveying of another individual's experience. This is what makes an individual protagonist indispensable to a narrative. It is a large part of the reason that

Sergei Eisenstein's experiments with a collective protagonist, that is, the masses as hero, were generally unsuccessful.[1]

The advantage of storytelling is that it is a re-presentation of *experience*, and as such involves our emotions. Our emotions, seated in the old brain (the part of our brain we share with other mammals) predate our newfound capacity for abstraction, which was conferred upon us by our recent acquisition of a much larger cortex. Stories are structured in such a way as to facilitate channeling new information through the old (and more basic) mechanisms of learning through interaction with the environment (that is, through experience), thereby allowing us to feel and to care about their content. The power of storytelling is in the re-presentation of experience at once to our intellect and to our emotions.

The cinema co-opts this power by presenting a surrogate reality structured as narrative. Narrative cinema accesses our primitive (old brain) emotional capacities and allows us to bring abstract, intellectual, cultural understandings into our experience of, and feelings about, the fictional events of a movie. Such a concept of the power of cinema opposes the notion of "absorption" as something insidious that will keep us from thinking about a movie. The more powerful and interesting possibility is that through cinema ideas can become incorporated into feelings.

The Organization of a Story

The teller of a story carefully structures it in terms of a hierarchy of cause and effect relationships in order to limit the number of possible interpretations by a receiver of the story. The receiver of the story is therefore not free to assign arbitrary meanings to the events. Jean Mandler has set out to discover just how stories are structured and understood. The traditional folktale provides a useful example:

> The great advantage of traditional stories for psychological study, in fact, is their relatively rigid for-

mats. The same kinds of structures appear over and over again in the folktales of the world. Thus, it was possible to uncover the structure that they do have, and to investigate how people incorporate that structure into their knowledge systems. The relative lack of variation in the formats of stories from the oral tradition provides us with an easy avenue for the exploration of schema formation and use.[2]

Although we should not underestimate the value of cause-effect relationships for limiting the number of possible meanings of a story, a schema, an organized representation of the content of the story, such as Mandler describes, in practice "provides such a strong basis for coherence that one can leave out all explicit reference to causal and temporal connections from the surface structure, yet leave the narrative comprehensible; the schema itself provides the connectives missing from the surface."[3] If the story is short, we simply rearrange the parts to fit our schema. If it is a long and complex story, however, we may not be able to follow it if the parts are presented in the wrong order. Experimental research indicates, in fact, that as material is presented out of sequential order and one is asked to hold events or ideas in memory for longer periods of time before they are resolved or connected to other events or ideas, one's capacity for recall suffers.[4]

This raises an interesting question: If presenting material out of order makes it more difficult to recall, then why do we do it? Why are stories not always told in chronological order? The reason is, of course, that in some cases stories may create a more dramatic effect, greater emotional impact if rearranged. For example, suspense may be heightened by withholding certain events until the end.

The Teller of the Story

Sometimes the experience of a movie is that of walking through the diegesis and discovering its events as they appear before us. We do not feel the presence of an organizer or teller behind the construction of the fictional world that we inhabit; the experience is ours, and if there is a story to be told then it is ours to tell. At other times we *are* aware that we are being told a story, and we crane our necks to get a better view of the storyteller. We want to know his intentions, his point of view, his motive for telling the story as he does.

With a live storyteller, we judge his intentions by his facial expressions, the tone of his voice, his body movements, and as he leads us into the fictional world that he is creating before our very eyes, we trust or distrust him, believe or disbelieve what he tells us, based upon our assessment of his character. In a movie, we are denied the physical presence of the storyteller, and we must come to know his character and judge his intentions in some other way. Sometimes, of course, we are given an on-screen narrator, and we are free to subject him to the same scrutiny as a live storyteller, which may result in our learning something of *his* character, but our efforts to perceive the intentions of *the* teller of the story are ultimately thwarted, for we know that this on-screen narrator is himself a construction of the master storyteller.

The question arises as to whether it is necessary for us as film viewers to make a judgment about the master storyteller's intentions at all. Do we need to know his relationship to the story in order to fully experience the movie? Do we need a storyteller at all? This is the paradox inherent in filmic narrative. We know that a story is being told to us, yet we experience the events of a motion picture *directly*, and the experience is not another's, but our own.

One can argue that the quest for such an implied author is pure folly or that the construction of such an entity is usually unnecessary. An argument for the former is that such a storyteller does not actually exist; we are not talking about the director or producer or writer or even a team of people who may have actually worked to make the movie. The storyteller in a motion picture is of necessity a disembodied persona who tells the story, an abstraction of our invention.

The argument for the latter has been forcefully stated by David Bordwell: "As for the implied author, this construct adds nothing to our understanding of filmic narration. No trait we could assign to an implied author of a film could not more simply be ascribed to the narration itself: it sometimes suppresses information, it often restricts our knowledge, it generates curiosity, it creates a tone, and so on."[5] The conclusion we draw from such arguments might be that we should avoid altogether the assumption of a storyteller in connection with a movie. But it is not easy to dismiss the idea of such a storyteller, and Bordwell, of course, recognized this reality; his advice is that "we ought not to proliferate theoretical entities without need." Instead, he suggests that it is better "to give the narrational process the power to signal under certain circumstances that the spectator should construct a narrator."[6] When called upon to do so, construction of a narrator (and subsequent attribution of intention and disposition to that narrator) is not a difficult or extraordinary task for the viewer. As we discussed in the context of attribution theory, we construct personalities and attribute disposition and motivation to other people every day.

An ecological perspective may once again prove useful in describing the circumstances under which a narrator should be constructed. As both Gombrich and Gibson observed, we are by nature active information seekers, and we are efficient in that activity. We do not seek information at random; we seek information that can lead to clarification of our comprehension in preparation for informed action. When we are viewing a movie, our mechanism of attention is much too efficient to concern itself with phantom entities that serve no immediate need. And *need* is the key. When the flow of events on the screen leads us to the awareness of being told a story, we begin our active search for the teller in order to clarify his relationship to the story so that we may clarify our own. For although we can, and do, ignore much of the information available to us, we are fervent seekers of clarification.

The motion picture *Stevie* (1978) is interesting with regard to storytelling in general and storytellers in particular, for it is both a story about a storyteller (the British writer Stevie Smith) and a complex story in its own right offering two, perhaps three, onscreen narrators. If we are to construct yet another narrator, we must endow him or her with a penchant for reflexive story construction.

The structure of the film involves a framing device consisting of an on-screen narrator played by Trevor Howard but identified simply as "The Man." The main story, the life of Stevie Smith, is then told in chronological order through flashbacks. The temporal order makes the story surprisingly easy to follow given its other complexities.

Although the film embodies many structural intricacies worthy of our exploration, let us consider two instances that seem to cry out for the construction of an extra-diegetic narrator: If the viewer were not already seeking clarification concerning the intentions of the storyteller there is a moment when "The Man," who for more than half the movie has served in the formal capacity of narrator, suddenly appears at Stevie's door and walks into the space and time occupied by Stevie and the other characters and begins taking part in the action. Viewers witnessing the man jump from one level of narrative to another become aware of the intentional manipulation of narrative structure. At this point, the viewers do the same thing they would do were they not caught up in the diegetic world of the movie: they seek further clarification. They ask who is doing the manipulation and what his intentions are. Is the storyteller a madman bent upon leading one toward insanity or is he kindly imparting wisdom? Even the experienced or educated viewer needs clarification.

There is another moment at the end of the film when we return to the empty room of Stevie's house on Avondale Road. "The Man," once again in his role of narrator, tells us of Stevie's last days in the hospital and of her death. Stevie appears in the scene, seated in her aunt's chair, and narrates her own letter writing, exhibiting the same speech difficulties she presumably experienced at the time of writing the letter. "The Man" walks over behind her chair. We see his hands on the back of the chair behind Stevie, and the camera tilts up to his face, thereby excluding Stevie from the shot. He concludes his story and leaves the room, turning off the light and closing the door behind him. The narrator has just walked out of the movie, but the camera remains and pans back to the chair where Stevie sat, showing us that it is now empty. But who shows us the empty chair?

The master storyteller has, it seems, had the last word. In fact, the struggle for narrational dominance is a major theme of the movie. Early on, Stevie comments upon her disagreement with a BBC producer about his telling of her story, overtly introducing the theme of a conflict over narrational dominance. The rest of the film can be seen as a three-way struggle for the narrator's role between the character Stevie, "The Man," and the film's implied storyteller (the two instances here described being times when the "master teller" attains dominance).

Returning to our consideration of the circumstances under which a viewer needs to construct a teller of the movie story, we have but to ask what the options are for a viewer confronted with the two moments described from *Stevie*. There are not many. One can either set about ascribing intentions and character to a presumed storyteller and thereby gain clarification of the teller's relationship to the events in the story and ultimately the viewer's relationship, or one can seek refuge in the certain knowledge that it is only a movie and abort all efforts toward clarification. An experienced viewer may do the former, a less experienced viewer the latter. Here the analogy to Neisser's chess board is relevant. But there is even more variability in movies than in chess games. Not every film engages all the schemata for film viewing that an experienced viewer may possess. And some films require schemata that not all viewers have bothered to acquire.

What One Takes Away

What we feel during the viewing of a film is the result of moment-to-moment concern for the characters for whom we perceive the affordances in the diegetic world, but it is not necessarily what we walk away with. What is it that we take away from a film? What do we remember?

Neisser notes that psychology has recently developed new definitions of the kinds of things we remember. Just as perceptual psychologists once assumed that we begin with discrete units of sensory data and process them in order to arrive at a percept, cognitive psychologists have assumed that we remember specific, personally experienced events. Now perceptual psychologists are talking about larger units of perception in an ecological context, and cognitive psychologists have come to understand that we remember not only specific events, but also facts, story structures, routines (or scripts), and spatial layouts.

Perhaps most surprising is the discovery that specific events have no privileged place in memory. Children, for instance, are better at remembering "scripts" than the individual episodes of which they are composed. This process is usually described as the transforming of one type of mental representation into another—converting stored memories of several episodes into a "script" that includes the properties they have in common. But Neisser prefers to describe the process more ecologically: the child's memory is simply more attuned to one class of memoria (repeated sequences) than to others (unique episodes).

The same logic would explain why specific episodes can be entirely forgotten, while the generic memory persists. The more similar the episodes, the more likely that their common structure will become salient and their individual characteristics forgotten. We therefore remember not only episodes, but also enduring and recurrent experiences. Individual episodes have no privileged status in memory; it is at least as natural to remember extended situations or typical patterns.[7]

We may recall that Mandler said our schema for stories is hierarchical, ordered, and abstract. Similarly, Neisser suggests that memory, too, is a matter of hierarchical organization—events are nested within larger structures.

> We perceive and remember events at many levels
> of analysis. We remember conferences, talks, and sen-
> tences; lasting personal relationships, special eve-
> nings, and pregnant moments; graduate school years,
> particular seminars, memorable remarks. The organi-
> zation of autobiographical memory evidently parallels
> the hierarchical organization of the remembered
> events themselves. Mental representations . . . are
> nested in one another just as events are.[8]

The pervasiveness of hierarchical organization extends to perception itself. On this point, Neisser cites Gibson: "Environmental sequences commonly have cycles embedded in larger
cycles, that is, *nested* events . . . Units are nested within other
units. And the remarkable fact is that both the superordinate
and the subordinate events can be perceived."[9]

An equally remarkable fact, Neisser notes, is that both superordinate and subordinate events can be remembered. But
long-term memory seems to favor the superordinate units,
the larger event, the overall structure. Put another way, all
levels of memory are subject to forgetting. The lower levels
of the hierarchy are more vulnerable than the higher ones.
As the Gestalt psychologists might say, the whole is more
memorable than the parts. This seems to be true of biographi-
cal memory, of recall of a story, and of what we take away
from the viewing of a film.

Beyond what is usually thought of as memory, we may
ask whether there are other consequences of watching a film.
Do we take away anything else from the experience; are we
changed by it? I have said that the schemata we bring to films
are those we bring to other experiences in the world, and
when the film viewing experience modifies those schemata
(as all perceptual and cognitive cycles do) it has in some way
changed the way we will interact with the world.

Of course, there are some film-specific schemata. Professional film viewers (like professional chess players) have developed elaborate film viewing schemata. And as we view a

film that stretches our capacity for understanding, our schemata are modified accordingly. But our schemata relating specifically to film are ultimately less important than those relating to other things. Movies have a major impact precisely because they have the capacity to change the way we think about things other than movies, things in the real world.

I have maintained that film is a framed activity, set apart from reality and distinguished from it unequivocally. And not knowing the difference between the framed event (the fiction) and reality constitutes insanity. However, we may become aware of some elements in common between the fictional world and our world. Those elements are most likely to be of the superordinate category favored by long-term memory and can be very abstract. These elements, in a sense, transcend the frame and directly affect the way we view our world. For example, *Mean Streets*, *Taxi Driver*, *Chinatown*, *Blue Velvet*, and *Silence of the Lambs* are films that have the capacity to change one's basic schema of the balance of good and evil in the world—not in movies, but in the world. One may feel, in the aftermath of having seen these films, that evil transcends the frame and permeates the world outside the theater.

Our viewing experience is a form of vigorous mental play. The activity is framed and set apart from ordinary experience, yet it takes place in a surrogate world that we can see and hear. We seek information about this world using the same perceptual strategies that we use every day. We sort out its physical, social, and psychological complexities as we would those of the real physical world. Throughout our interaction, we feel real emotions and acquire real insights, and at the end we step back from the frame and walk away more hopeful, perhaps, or more cynical or wiser in some way, in some degree changed forever by the experience.

There is yet another wrinkle in the process of memory that is particularly relevant to motion picture viewing. In the recall of past events, as has been noted, our grasp of the overall situation may remain intact but our exact recollection of the specific details seems to slip with the passage of time.

Loss of detail in memory often puts us in an odd situation. We may remember an overall event, perhaps well enough to infer its more specific characteristics, but we do not remember those characteristics themselves. That is why memory is so vulnerable to unintended distortion, and why it often seems "true" even when it is false. We can never do full justice to what Spence has called historical truth, because what really happened was too rich for anyone's memory to preserve. But it is relatively easy to remember events in a way that is accurate with respect to some overall characteristic of the situation; such a recollection always has some degree of validity even if it suggests nested details that are by no means accurate themselves. In the end the episode-as-remembered may have only the kind of validity that Spence called "narrative truth": it will be truthful in some respects and yet very far from historically accurate.[10]

Can it be that what Spence calls narrative truth Edward Branigan calls fictional truth? Can we see the episodes of fiction as just such episodes that point to the larger structure, the overall event that gave rise to them? Perhaps so.

Branigan's concept of fiction as a partially determined referent is closely related to the nonspecific but illustrative nature of Neisser's "episodes-as-remembered." Branigan suggests that

a person in a photograph can be simultaneously both specific and (fictionally) nonspecific in the same way that a photograph of a tiger in a dictionary can be both a specific tiger and many tigers.... When a film is experienced fictionally, reference is not to the *profilmic* event in which a set is decorated and an actor given direction, but rather to a *postfilmic* event in which patterns are discovered through active perceiving that affects the overall structure of our knowledge.[11]

Often "episodes-as-remembered" are accompanied by visual images. That is, these generic memories are accompanied by specific images. Neisser suggests that these mental images do not function primarily as carriers of specific information, but serve to "illustrate" the memory. Even a never-experienced or impossible view of an event may illustrate a general recollection particularly well. If this is the way our minds structure memories of our personal experiences, is it not likely to be the way in which it structures memories of fictional experiences as well?

Summary

I have drawn a parallel between Neisser's view that the mind uses narrative truth as opposed to historical truth in remembering the events of our lives and Branigan's contention that fictional truth arises from the structuring of a series of partially determined referents. In doing so, I am informed by Branigan's admonition that "despite the fact that fiction often deals in exotic subjects, a theory of fiction should be built upon a careful examination of our ordinary ways of thinking and our everyday abilities."[12] Here he is in excellent company. Fritz Heider, David Marr, and J. J. Gibson voiced similar insights. Heider advocated the study of "common-sense" psychology because it is by means of such a psychology that we go about every day interpreting the actions of other people and predicting what they will do next. Our methods may not meet the criteria of science. (We often make snap decisions, we judge by appearances, and we rely on stereotypes.) Nevertheless, these are the methods we employ in our daily affairs, and these are the methods we bring to the viewing of movies.

Heider was quick to point out that common-sense psychology is neither foolish nor arbitrary, but instead provides us with a systematic and veridical basis for our social interaction. And David Marr, in discussing the perspectives that must be satisfied in developing a theory of vision, warned against

overlooking that of the "plain man": "He knows what it is to
see, and unless the bones of one's arguments and theories
roughly correspond to what this person knows to be true at
first hand, one will probably be wrong."[13] J. J. Gibson, too,
was extremely skeptical of theories that failed to take into
account our common experience in the world. He began with
the observation that "the habitat of all animals, as far as we
know, is the planet earth"[14] and built his theory of perception
upon the manifest adaptions of earthly creatures to an earthly
environment.

An ecologically based theory of film would elevate ordinary perception, ordinary thinking, and ordinary feeling, for
the world of the fictional motion picture, as it has developed,
is constructed of the ordinary materials (places, personalities,
clothing, bits of relationships, and so forth) that we deal with
every day in the real world. This is why, unlike the difficulty
of learning to read, the ability to view motion pictures is
readily acquired. There is no special alphabet, no special language of film. We see and hear the characters and events of
motion pictures directly.

That we see and hear the characters and events of a motion
picture directly is, of course, the explanation of the narrative
paradox in motion pictures. That is, we know that motion
pictures are constructed narratives, and yet our experience is
often that of *discovering* places and events and relationships
on our own. Because we as spectators are able to explore the
fictional world directly by means of the complex cinematic
illusion, we have no need for a storyteller until the story being
told becomes self-referential, and we suddenly realize that we
are being told a story. Then we quite naturally and predictably
go through the process of attributing character and motive
to the narrator of the movie story as we would for any teller
of a story. Such self-referentiality is usually avoided by movie-
makers because it works against the potential for experiencing
the fictional events of the movie directly, which is, after all,
the special edge that motion pictures hold over other forms
of storytelling.

10
Conclusion

Remember our friend, the attorney, who wanted to know why a movie seems so real, and why the spokes of a wheel turn in reverse? He is a veteran moviegoer, and his assessment of movie viewing is similar to the judgment offered by Hugo Munsterberg almost nine decades ago: "It is a superb enjoyment which no other art can furnish us."[1] And he, like Munsterberg, wants to know the status of his experience. His absorption in the fictional world of the film seems to require little effort on his part; it seems to be a triumph of mind over matter, and indeed "the pictures [do] roll on with the ease of musical tones."[2] But our attorney is not a trusting man; he is suspicious by profession, if not by nature, and he knows that appearances can deceive. It is not that he demands a fundamental literalism, that he seeks some simplistic distinction between truth and fiction. He is, after all, a learned man, and he knows that there can be truth *in* fiction. No, it is not the relationship between truth and fiction that he seeks; it is the relationship between his experience of a movie and his experience of reality in general that leaves him bewildered.

When he views a movie, he is buoyed up by a strong sense of the reality; he does not question the status of the experience until something incongruent with normal perception occurs, as when in the midst of one of his favorite John Ford movies the spokes in the wheels of a western stagecoach come to a stop and then slowly begin to rotate in the reverse direction.[3] Suddenly the spell is broken, the trickery behind the illusion is revealed, and our usually unperturbable attorney is thrown into a state of confusion concerning the status of his experience. He will not be mollified by a superficial and essentially mystifying attempt to explain what has happened in terms of breaking the diegesis and revealing the work. He is un-impressed with the argument that he has been set free from the hex of absorption and allowed to glimpse a bit of that otherwise most elusive of phenomena—truth. Our jaded bar-rister demands a better accounting of his experience, and I have tried to provide it; though, as I feared from the begin-ning, the effort has filled an entire book.

So how much do we know about the interface between motion pictures and the human mind? It turns out that the scientific study of the human mind has so far yielded only a rough sketch of the entire project, and our knowledge at pre-sent is fragmentary, but some insights have been achieved that can inform our understanding of motion pictures. At the top of our list is the insight that all perception, all cognition, is referenced to the environment in which it developed. Next, there is the insight that the mind is modular, that it functions more like a roomful of PCs all interconnected than a main-frame with work stations, thus allowing the processing of several streams of information and rather direct cross-check-ing for veridicality. There is also the insight that perception is a very active process and functions as though there were program-like structures called schemata that guide the search for information in an ongoing process of exploration and modification. And there is the insight that the brain is a very slow processor, and that internal short-cuts have been devel-oped in a number of areas, from visual perception to person perception and character attribution, that enable processing to proceed at a rate fast enough to allow for the possibility of acting upon the information so obtained. But the increased processing speed has been gained at a price: the opening up of the possibility of illusions.

The postulates here proposed are the following: first, that from the viewer's side, a motion picture is an illusion (with illusion defined as nonveridical perception); second, that the viewer voluntarily enters into the diegetic world of a movie by means of a genetically endowed capacity for play; and third, that the motion picture is a surrogate for the physical world (a surrogate being an actual substitute for something else, as distinguished from an arbitrary symbol that stands for something else). Let me illustrate each of these postulates briefly.

Imagine, if you will, an ancient Arab philosopher who has pitched his tent before an oasis in the desert and who now sits inside the tent at midday to avoid the searing heat and blinding brightness of the desert sun. As his eyes adapt to the relative darkness, he catches in the corner of his eye a movement in the back of his tent. He turns his head and looks more closely. In a patch of light, he sees a bird in flight that has come to drink from the spring, which is there also, and the lone palm tree. It is all there, the entire oasis is there on the back wall of his tent, but it is upside down. It looks so real, an upside down oasis! He reaches out his hand to touch the vision, to see if it is real, and it disappears from the wall. But there it is on his hand. He cannot feel the tree or the bird or the water with his fingers, so he lowers his hand and sees the image again on the wall, steady and persistent, and it is animated with the movement of the bird as it drinks from the spring. The wise philosopher looks about the tent for the cause of this apparition and sees the cone of light emanating from a small hole in the front of the tent. Opening the tent flap slightly, he observes that straight lines could be drawn from the tree, the spring, the bird to their images upon the back of the tent. He concludes that straight rays of light link the image directly in time and space with the real oasis before his tent.

We of course recognize the tent with a hole in it as a *camera obscura* in which the hole functions as a lens, in that it allows only the rays of light which accurately line up with the hole to pass through to the back wall of the tent. Such a coherent bundle of light rays results in a coherent, and therefore sharp, image. Is the image an illusion? To answer this question we must ask whether the philosopher's perception is veridical.

Certainly his perception of the image on the tent wall is veridical, that is, he correctly perceives that it is an image on the tent wall. But does the image on the tent wall allow the philosopher a veridical perception of the oasis? His perception that the oasis exists in the present time, and that the bird is moving about the spring drinking water is accurate enough. He could act upon that information; he could get a drink of water for himself or hold the bird in his hand, except for the fact that the oasis is displaced. It appears upside down on the back wall of his tent when in reality it is outside in front of his tent. He cannot drink from the spring nor hold the bird he sees; his perception is nonveridical. The illusion is one of spatial displacement. (The illusion of ourselves standing behind the surface of a mirror is also a matter of displacement.)

Now let us suppose that the philosopher could have made a motion picture of the oasis and left it for us to view. We project the film and we see the spring, the palm tree, and the restless bird that flies from the tree to the spring and drinks the cool water. The image we see upon our screen is the same as the one projected upon the rear wall of his tent. (We could even turn the projector upside down.) Ours is an illusion of both temporal and spatial displacement (long ago and far away). And there is another illusion involved. We see the bird move about even though we know that a motion picture is made up of a succession of still pictures that are projected one at a time while the film is intermittently held stationary. The motion of the bird seen by the philosopher was real motion, ours is apparent motion—an illusion. We conclude therefore that a motion picture provokes many illusions in our perception; there are illusions nested within illusions.

But of course my account of the Arab philosopher is fictional.[4] Much of the information contained in the visual and auditory arrays generated by a movie concerns a fictional world. The spectator's access to and full participation in that world is made possible by a genetically endowed capacity for play. We are by nature playful creatures, and when we play we enter into fictional worlds having their own rules, whether we are playing hopscotch on the sidewalk, reading a novel, or viewing a movie. It is not a matter of suspending disbelief; it is a matter of framing, of having the capacity to see things inside the frame as being of a different order than things outside the frame. In reading, it is not enough to know the words, nor even to process the language in all its complexity. One must cross a threshold of fantasy; one must experience the events of a novel in the fullness allowed by play. The same is true of one's experience of a motion picture.

Those of us who have had the experience of checking our answer print at a lab know that it is possible to view the entire motion picture and judge the lightness and darkness and color of the images as well as the quality of the sound track, to check the cuts from shot to shot, to see the characters, and to check their skin tones and costumes without ever committing ourselves to entering into the fictional world. Clearly, one must frame the events of a movie in order to experience it fully, for nested within the physical arrays presented to our perception is a fictional world of people and events that we must enter. But the access to the fictional world of a motion picture is easy and generally available to everyone, though none of us can remain firmly rooted in its reality; we are involuntarily pulled and pushed, in and out of it.

Because motion pictures can be constructed of the stuff of everyday experience, they can function as a surrogate for the physical world, not in the way that arbitrary symbols such as words may stand for physical objects, but as an actual substitute for the thing itself. This is possible because, unlike a word, a photograph actually offers some of the affordances of the actual object. As a practical matter, still photographs, motion pictures, and video images are so effective as surrogates that in almost every field, from astrophysics to social psychology, they are employed in research situations without apology. They are not employed as symbols; they are simply substituted for the real physical object in the interest of convenience, and they are as satisfactory in a practical sense because while not offering all the affordances of the actual object or event, they offer the requisite ones.

A most intriguing question arises at this point. Is it possible to interact with a substitute or surrogate, something known to be less than the real thing, and yet derive very real experience from that interaction? Harry F. Harlow addressed this question in his work with infant rhesus monkeys at the Primate Laboratory at the University of Wisconsin.[5] In his investigation of the infant-mother relationship Harlow employed substitute or surrogate mothers. The surrogates he used were welded-wire cylindrical forms designed to afford opportunities for one or more of a variety of activities for the infants, such as nursing, clinging, or rocking. The version of the surrogate mother overwhelmingly preferred by the infant monkeys was a cloth-covered one that provided a soft surface for cuddling and clinging.

Harlow was interested in determining which of those activities was most central in establishing the infant's affection for the mother, but for our purpose the critical information from Harlow's studies is the effect produced by interaction with a surrogate rather than a real mother. The experience produced real behaviors and presumably real emotions on the part of the infants.

While a cloth-covered cylindrical form in the infant monkey's cage is not a live monkey and cannot be actively nurturant, it allows for certain critical needs of the infant (such as pressing, rubbing, and clinging) to be fulfilled. Gibson would say that the real mother and the surrogate offer some of the same affordances—precisely those Harlow isolated as being critical for bonding. And this is the significant point: the feelings engendered by contact with the surrogate mother are real. They affect the infant's sense of well-being, his "view of the world," and his personality; they directly affect his development. The experience with a surrogate mother was found to be equivalent to experience with a real mother: "All the objective tests we have been able to devise agree in showing that the infant monkey's relationship to its surrogate mother is a full one. Comparison with the behavior of infant monkeys raised by their real mothers confirms this view. . . . The deep and abiding bond between mother and child appears to be essentially the same, whether the mother is real or a cloth surrogate."[6]

It is in this sense that a film functions as a surrogate for reality at several levels. It is clear to viewers that it is "only a movie," but just as knowledge of a visual illusion does not prevent its being seen, so too the film-as-surrogate-reality does not prevent the viewers' experience from engendering real feelings and thoughts that will confirm, support, or undermine aspects of their view of reality. The danger in a thriller is not real; the fear we feel for the character in danger is. The tragedy in a movie's narrative is not real; the empathy and sorrow we feel are.

In the end, my learned friend, the answer to your question is this: a movie seems so real because we see the events and hear the sounds of its fictional world *directly*. Of course the motion picture is an illusion, or a set of nested illusions, and the illusions hold only as long as they meet the conditions demanded by our perceptual systems. The spell can be rather easily broken, as it is when spoked wheels appear to rotate in reverse because the film itself, as an artifact of the way it is produced, presents to the visual system information for backward motion rather than forward motion. And even though we *know* that the wheels are in fact rotating in a forward direction, we have no capacity for entering this information into our perception. Our various capacities for interacting with the illusions of a motion picture seem to be finite, discrete, and bounded. They are part of our rich biological heritage, a legacy of the relentless forces of evolution. And the key to understanding these capacities is to see them as integral to the ecology in which they developed.

With a theory of film constructed upon such a basis, that

is, upon an understanding of our capacities and a recognition of their inherent boundaries, we can legitimately hope to account for the complex set of nested illusions that constitute a motion picture. Unlike the free-floating film theories of the past two decades, an ecologically-based cognitive film theory, by dint of its reliance upon research findings adherent to scientific method, would have a small purchase on reality itself, much as a clam, though elegant and complete in its own right, nevertheless places one tiny foot squarely against the world.

Notes
Selected Bibliography
Index

Notes

1. Introduction

1. Hugo Munsterberg, *The Photoplay: A Psychological Study* (New York: D. Appleton, 1916; reprint, *The Film: A Psychological Study*, New York: Dover Publications, 1970).

2. For a more complete discussion of the psychoanalytic/Marxist paradigm in film theory see Noel Carroll, *Mystifying Movies* (New York: Columbia Univ. Press, 1988).

3. See David Bordwell, *Narration in the Fiction Film* (Madison: Univ. of Wisconsin Press, 1985) and Carroll, *Mystifying Movies*.

4. Karl R. Popper, "Truth, Rationality, and the Growth of Scientific Knowledge," in *Philosophical Problems of Science and Technology*, ed. Alexandros C. Michalos (Boston: Allyn and Bacon, 1974), 78.

5. See Murray Krieger, "The Ambiguities of Representation and Illusion: An E. H. Gombrich Retrospective," *Critical Inquiry* 11,2 (Dec. 1984): 181–94; and E. H. Gombrich, "Representation and Misrepresentation," *Critical Inquiry* 11,2 (Dec. 1984): 195–201.

6. Hugo Munsterberg, "Why We Go to the 'Movies'," *Cosmopolitan*, Dec. 1915, 31.

2. Toward an Ecology of Cinema

1. Gregory Bateson, *Steps to An Ecology of Mind* (New York: Ballantine Books, 1972), xv–xvi.

2. Bateson, *Steps*, xii.

3. James E. Cutting, "Perceptual Artifacts and Phenomena: Gibson's Role in the 20th Century," in *Foundations of Perceptual Theory*, ed. Sergio C. Masin (Amsterdam: Elsevier Science Publishers, 1993), 236.

4. James J. Gibson, *The Ecological Approach to Visual Perception* (Boston: Houghton Mifflin, 1979), 16.

5. Julian Hochberg, "Gestalt Theory," in *The Oxford Companion to the Mind*, ed. Richard L. Gregory (Oxford: Oxford Univ. Press, 1987), 288.

6. The schism runs through the middle of most disciplines that make up cognitive psychology. For example, in Artificial Intelligence (AI) there is the *symbolic processing* approach and the *situated action*

approach, with proponents of the latter generally claiming lineage
to Gibson, even though one might question whether there is sufficient
appreciation of the biological (as opposed to merely environmental)
basis of Gibson's theory in that claim.

7. James J. Gibson, *The Senses Considered as Perceptual Systems*
(Boston: Houghton Mifflin, 1966), 26.

8. Vicki Bruce and Patrick R. Green, *Visual Perception: Physiology,
Psychology and Ecology*, 2d ed. (Hillsdale, N.J.: Lawrence Erlbaum
Associates, 1990), 382.

9. Ulric Neisser, "What is Ordinary Memory the Memory Of?"
in *Remembering Reconsidered*, ed. Ulric Neisser and Eugene Winograd
(Cambridge: Cambridge Univ. Press, 1988), 360.

10. J. J. Gibson, *Ecological Approach*, 198–200.

11. For a discussion of evolution from a contemporary perspective, see John Rennie, "DNA's New Twists," *Scientific American* 26,3
(Mar. 1993): 122–32.

12. Jean Baptiste Pierre Antoine de Monet de Lamarck, *Philosophie zoologique* (Paris: Dentu, 1809; Weinheim: H. R. Englemann,
1960).

13. The fact that we can see better at night when we look slightly
to one side of an object rather than directly at it is accounted for in
part by the use of peripheral receptors that "sum" their outputs by
feeding into a single ganglion cell.

14. The organization of visual processing at a cellular level was
first described in detail by D. H. Hubel and T. N. Wiesel in their
landmark article, "Receptive Fields, Binocular Interaction, and Functional Architecture in the Cat's Visual Cortex," *Journal of Physiology*
160 (1962): 106–54.

15. J. J. Gibson, *Senses*, 26.

16. David Marr, *Vision* (New York: W. H. Freeman, 1982), 30.

17. Marr, *Vision*, 27–29.

18. Glyn W. Humphreys and Vicki Bruce, *Visual Cognition*
(Hillsdale, N.J.: Lawrence Erlbaum Associates, 1989), 105.

19. Vilayanur S. Ramachandran and Stuart M. Anstis, "The Perception of Apparent Motion," *Scientific American* 254,6 (June 1986):
102–9.

20. Ramachandran and Anstis, "Perception," 109.

3. Capacities and Strategies

1. Michael S. Gazzaniga, *Nature's Mind: The Biological Roots of
Thinking, Emotions, Sexuality, Language and Intelligence* (New York: Basic Books, 1992), 6.

2. Gazzaniga, *Nature's Mind*, 110.

3. Gazzaniga, *Nature's Mind*, 109.

4. Gazzaniga, *Nature's Mind*, 106.

5. Ernst H. Gombrich, *Art And Illusion: A Study in the Psychology of Pictorial Representation* (Princeton: Princeton Univ. Press, 1960).

6. Gombrich, *Art And Illusion*, 29.

7. Gombrich, *Art And Illusion*, 298.

8. For further reading on the controversy in psychology over the issue of direct perception, see Mark H. Bickhard and D. Michael Richie, *On the Nature of Representation* (New York: Praeger, 1983); Clair F. Michaels and Claudia Carello, *Direct Perception* (Englewood Cliffs, N.J.: Prentice Hall, 1981); Jerry Fodor and Zenon W. Pylyshyn, "How Direct is Visual Perception?," *Cognition* 9 (1981): 139–96; Shiman Ullman, "Against Direct Perception," *The Behavioral and Brain Sciences* 3 (1980): 373–81.

9. See especially Ernst H. Gombrich, "Representation and Misrepresentation," *Critical Inquiry* 11,2 (Dec. 1984): 195–201.

10. J. J. Gibson, *Senses*, 279–80.

11. Ulric Neisser, *Cognition and Reality* (New York: W. H. Freeman, 1976), 180–81.

12. Neisser, *Cognition and Reality*, 182

13. Neisser, *Cognition and Reality*, 20.

14. Neisser, *Cognition and Reality*, 77.

15. J. J. Gibson, *Ecological Approach*, 205.

16. Joseph D. Anderson et al., "Binocular Integration in Line Rivalry," *Bulletin of the Psychonomic Society* 11,6 (1978): 399–402.

17. For a general introduction to chaotic systems in relation to perception, see Walter J. Freeman, "The Physiology of Perception," *Scientific American* 264,2 (Feb. 1991): 78–85.

18. John E. Hummel and Irving Biederman, "Dynamic Binding: A Basis for the Representation of Shape by Neural Networks," in *The Twelfth Annual Conference of the Cognitive Science Society* (Hillsdale, N.J.: Lawrence Erlbaum Associates, 1990), 614–22.

19. See Joseph D. Anderson, "An Investigation of Binocular Integration in Rivalry Phenomena" (Ph.D. diss., Univ. of Iowa, 1974).

20. Ulric Neisser, "From Direct Perception to Conceptual Structure," in *Concepts and Conceptual Development*, ed. Ulric Neisser (Cambridge: Cambridge Univ. Press, 1987), 11–24.

21. Neisser, "From Direct Perception," 14.

22. Neisser, "From Direct Perception," 13.

4. Some Problems Reconsidered

1. For more information on the development of technology in the fields of film and television, see Raymond Fielding, ed. *A Tech-*

nological History of Motion Pictures and Television (Berkeley: Univ. of California Press, 1967).

2. Thomas Armat, "My Part in the Development of the Motion Picture Projector," in *A Technological History of Motion Pictures and Television*, ed. Raymond Fielding (Berkeley: Univ. of California Press, 1967), 22.

3. Raymond Fielding, "Accounting Practices in the Early American Motion Picture Industry," *Historical Journal of Film, Radio and Television* 12,2 (1992): 18.

4. Edward W. Kellogg, "History of Sound Motion Pictures," in *A Technological History of Motion Pictures and Television*, ed. Raymond Fielding (Berkeley: Univ. of California Press, 1967), 182.

5. Thomas Armat argues persuasively that important differences existed between cameras and projectors. See Armat, "My Part."

6. There is more than one method for doing such a conversion from film to video. According to A. G. Jensen, this was the way the problem was initially solved. See A. G. Jensen, "The Evolution of Modern Television," in *A Technological History of Motion Pictures and Television*, ed. Raymond Fielding (Berkeley: Univ. of California Press, 1967), 246.

7. Paul Kolers, *Aspects Motion Perception*, International Series of Monographs in Experimental Psychology, vol. 16 (Oxford: Pergamon Press, 1972), 39.

8. Marguerite Biederman-Thorson, John Thorson, and G. David Lange, "Apparent Movement Due to Closely Spaced Sequentially Flashed Dots in the Human Peripheral Field of Vision," *Vision Research* 11 (1971): 897.

9. Oliver Braddick, "A Short Range Process in Apparent Motion," *Vision Research* 14 (1974): 519–26.

10. For further discussion of this point, see Stuart M. Anstis, "The Perception of Apparent Movement," *Philosophical Transactions of the Royal Society of London*, Series B, 290, 153–68; and Oliver J. Braddick and A. J. Allard, "Apparent Motion and the Motion Detector," in *Visual Psychophysics and Physiology*, ed. J. Armington, J. Krauskopf, and B. R. Wooten (New York: Academic Press), 417–26.

11. J. Timothy Petersik, "The Two-Process Distinction in Apparent Motion," *Psychological Bulletin* 106,1 (1989): 118.

12. Margaret Livingstone and David H. Hubel, "Segregation of Form, Color, Movement and Depth: Anatomy, Physiology and Perception," *Science* 240 (6 May 1988), 740–49.

13. Semir Zeki, "The Visual Image in Mind and Brain," *Scientific American*, 267,3 (Sept. 1992): 69–76.

14. For discussion of work done by Rudiger von der Heydt and

Esther Peterhans on the response of cells in V1 and V2 to illusory contours, see Zeki, "Visual Image," 76.

15. See Joseph D. Anderson and Barbara Fisher, "The Myth of Persistence of Vision," *Journal of the University Film Association*, 30,4 (Fall 1978): 3–8; Joseph D. Anderson and Barbara Anderson, "Motion Perception in Motion Pictures," in *The Cinematic Apparatus*, ed. S. Heath and T. de Lauretis (New York: St. Martin's Press, 1980), 76–95; and Joseph D. Anderson and Barbara Anderson, "The Myth of Persistence of Vision Revisited," *Journal of Film and Video* 45,1 (Spring 1993), 3–12.

16. Stuart M. Anstis, "Phi Movement as a Subtraction Process," *Vision Research* 10 (1970), 1419.

17. Bela Julesz, *Foundations of Cyclopean Perception* (Chicago: Univ. of Chicago Press, 1971).

18. Livingstone and Hubel, "Segregation," 748.

19. Kolers, *Aspects*, 36.

20. Hubel and Wiesel, "Receptive Fields," 106–54.

21. Livingstone and Hubel, "Segregation," 743.

22. James E. Cutting, "Rigidity in Cinema Seen from the Front Row, Side Aisle," *Journal of Experimental Psychology: Human Perception and Performance* 13,3 (1987): 323–34.

23. G. J. F. Smets, C. J. Overbeeke, and M. H. Stratmann, "Depth on a Flat Screen," *Perceptual and Motor Skills* 64 (1987): 1023–34.

24. Smets, Overbeeke, and Stratmann, "Depth," 1026.

25. Smets, Overbeeke, and Stratmann, "Depth," 1024.

26. For a detailed analysis of such computations, see James E. Cutting, *Perception with an Eye to Motion* (Cambridge: MIT Press, 1986).

27. Erwin Panofsky, "Perspective as Symbolic Form," translation of "Die Perspektive als symbolische Form" (Vortrage de Bibliothek, Warburg, vol. 4, 1924–25, pp. 258–330.) Photocopy of typescript, 18.

28. Jean-Louis Baudry, "Ideological Effects of the Basic Cinematographic Apparatus," *Film Quarterly* 18,2 (Winter 1974/75): 39–47.

29. For a more detailed discussion of this view of perspective and alternative views, see Carroll, *Mystifying Movies*, 127–146; and Bordwell, *Narration*, 104–10.

30. Livingstone and Hubel, "Segregation," 747.

31. Livingstone and Hubel, "Segregation," 747.

32. See Leo M. Hurvich and Dorthea Jameson, "An Opponent Process Theory of Color Vision," *Psychological Review* 64 (1957): 384–404; and Leo M. Hurvich and Dorthea Jameson, *The Perception of Brightness and Darkness* (Boston: Allyn and Bacon, 1966).

33. See Edwin H. Land, "The Retinex Theory of Color Vision,"

Scientific American 237,6 (Dec. 1977), 108–28; and Edwin H. Land, "Recent Advances in Retinex Theory," *Vision Research* 26,1 (1986): 7–21.

5. Sound and Image

1. *The Twelfth Annual Conference of the Cognitive Science Society* (Hillsdale, N.J.: Lawrence Erlbaum Associates, 1990), 1013.

2. See chaps. 9 and 10 of *Perception and Its Development*, ed. Anne D. Pick (Hillsdale, N.J.: Lawrence Erlbaum Associates, 1979).

3. Elizabeth S. Spelke, "Exploring Audible and Visible Events in Infancy," in *Perception and Its Development*, ed. Anne D. Pick (Hillsdale, N.J.: Lawrence Erlbaum Associates, 1979), 221–35.

4. N. O'Connor and B. Hermelin, "Coding Strategies of Normal and Handicapped Children," in *Intersensory Perception and Sensory Integration*, ed. R. D. Walk and H. L. Pick Jr. (New York: Plenum, 1981), 315–43.

5. See John E. Hummel and Irving Biederman, "Dynamic Binding: A Basis for the Representation of Shape by Neural Networks," in *The Twelfth Annual Conference of the Cognitive Science Society* (Hillsdale, N.J.: Lawrence Erlbaum Associates, 1990).

6. See Dominic W. Massaro, *Speech Perception by Eye and Ear: A Paradigm for Psychological Inquiry* (Hillsdale, N.J.: Lawrence Erlbaum Associates, 1987), 236–37.

7. It is interesting to note that in matters of space perception, visual localization seems to dominate localization in other sensory modes. For discussions of this phenomenon, see Lawrence E. Marks, *The Unity of the Senses: Interrelations among the Modalities* (New York: Academic Press, 1978), 29–32; and Albert S. Bregman, *Auditory Scene Analysis* (Cambridge: MIT Press, 1990), especially 181–84 and 290–91.

8. For further discussion of looming, see Bruce and Green, *Visual Perception*, especially 268–69 and 307–8.

9. For research on the cross-cultural perception of emotion, see Paul Ekman, Robert W. Levenson, and Wallace V. Friesen, "Autonomic Nervous System Activity Distinguishes among Emotions," *Science* 221 (16 Sept. 1983): 1208–10; Paul Ekman et al., "Universals and Cultural Differences in the Judgments of Facial Expressions of Emotion," *Journal of Personality and Social Psychology*, 53,4 (1987): 712–17; Paul Ekman and Maureen O'Sullivan, "The Role of Context in Interpreting Facial Expression," *Journal of Experimental Psychology: General* 117,1 (1988): 86–88; Paul Ekman and Wallace V. Friesen, *Unmasking the Face* (Englewood Cliffs, N.J.: Prentice-Hall, 1975); Carroll E. Izard, *The Face of Emotion* (New York: Appleton-Century-Crofts,

1971); John N. Bassili, "Emotion Recognition: The Role of Facial Movement and the Relative Importance of Upper and Lower Areas of the Face," *Journal of Personality and Social Psychology*, 37,11 (1979): 2049–58; Leonard B. Meyer, *Emotion and Meaning in Music* (Chicago: Univ. of Chicago Press, 1956); and Robert Plutchik, *Emotion: A Psychoevolutionary Synthesis* (New York: Harper and Row, 1980). For research on *sentics*, see Manfred Clynes, *Sentics: The Touch of Emotion* (New York: Doubleday, 1977); and James R. Evans and Manfred Clynes, eds. *Rhythm in Psychological, Linguistic and Musical Processes*, (Springfield: Charles C. Thomas, 1986).

10. See Eleanor J. Gibson, *Principles of Perceptual Learning and Development* (Englewood Cliffs, N.J.: Prentice-Hall, 1969); and J. J. Gibson, *Ecological Approach*.

11. See Marks, *Unity of the Senses*.

12. Note that in the world, the implications of the event are registered in terms of the potential consequences to the perceiving individual—that is, what does this mean *to me?*—whereas when the perceiver interfaces with a narrative film, the implications of the event are registered in terms of the potential consequences not necessarily to the viewer himself but to a fictional character. These "implications" are what J. J. Gibson in his ecological approach to perception calls *affordances*, which he asserts are perceived in the process of perception itself.

13. Bregman, *Auditory Scene Analysis*, 184.

14. Eugene Narmour, *The Analysis and Cognition of Basic Melodic Structures* (Chicago: Univ. of Chicago Press, 1990).

15. Narmour, *Analysis*, 64–66.

6. Continuity

1. J. J. Gibson, *Senses*, 253.

2. J. J. Gibson, *Ecological Approach*, 204.

3. Livingstone and Hubel, "Segregation," 740–49.

4. J. J. Gibson, *Ecological Approach*, 13.

5. J. J. Gibson, *Ecological Approach*, 14.

6. Renee Baillargeon, "Young Infants' Physical World" and Adele Diamond, "The Planning, Execution and Inhibition of Movement During Infancy" (papers presented at the Neonate Cognition Symposium, The Twelfth Annual Conference of the Cognitive Science Society). Abstracted in *The Twelfth Annual Conference of the Cognitive Science Society* (Hillsdale, N.J.: Lawrence Erlbaum Associates, 1990): 1015, 1016.

7. Ken Nakayama, "Visual Inference in the Perception of Oc-

cluded Surfaces," (paper presented at the Neonate Cognition Symposium, The Twelfth Annual Conference of the Cognitive Science Society). Abstracted in *The Twelfth Annual Conference of the Cognitive Science Society* (Hillsdale, N.J.: Lawrence Erlbaum Associates, 1990), 1019.

8. Roadrunner cartoons come to mind as excellent examples of filmic reconstitution: destruction and subsequent reconstitution of the coyote character is a common occurrence in these animated films. Such reconstitution is presumably acceptable to infants who are too young to watch cartoons and to older children who do watch them. Indeed, such reconstitution is perfectly comprehensible to us adults even though we know it is physically impossible. Nature apparently did not bother to hardwire our perception in such a regard.

9. For a more detailed discussion of visual masking and the role it plays in cinematic motion and editing techniques, see Anderson and Anderson, "Motion Perception," 76–95.

10. J. J. Gibson, *Ecological Approach*, 205.

11. Edward Branigan, *Narrative Comprehension and Film* (New York: Routledge, Chapman and Hall, 1992), 53.

12. Neisser, "Ordinary Memory," 368–69.

13. J. J. Gibson, *Ecological Approach*, 34.

14. The term *cognitive map* is used here in the nonsymbolic sense. For a discussion of the concept, see chap. 2.

7. Diegesis

1. *Diegesis* is used here and elsewhere in the book to refer to the film's fictional world, or more precisely, the world available to the senses of the characters in a fictional work (for it is through the characters that we, the viewers, interact with the fictional world). For more detailed discussion of the concept of diegesis, see Edward Branigan, *Narrrative Comprehension and Film* (New York: Routledge, Chapman and Hall 1992); and Edward Branigan, "Diegesis and Authorship in Film," *Iris* 7,4 (Fall 1986): 37–54.

2. For a good discussion of the classic work on orientation, see Irvin Rock, *An Introduction to Perception* (New York: Macmillan, 1975), 457–500.

3. The experience thus afforded is greater in a theater where the diegetic array fills most of the visual field and has little competition. The image on a television set in a lighted room in the midst of other objects simply does not offer the same affordance. One should see *Star Wars* in a theater for maximum effect.

4. Sue Parker Taylor, "Playing for Keeps," in *Play in Animals and Humans*, ed. Peter K. Smith (New York: Basil Blackwell, 1984), 273.

5. Michael J. Ellis, *Why People Play* (Englewood Cliffs, N.J.: Prentice-Hall, 1973), 47.

6. Ellis, *Why People Play*, 89. For further discussion of the Reticulate Arousal System, see Ellis, 89–91.

7. Ellis, *Why People Play*, 92.

8. Ellis, *Why People Play*, 87.

9. Ellis, *Why People Play*, 87.

10. Gombrich, *Art and Illusion*, 303.

11. Ellis, *Why People Play*, 95.

12. Paul Martin, "The Whys and Wherefores of Play in Cats," in *Play in Animals and Humans*, ed. Peter K. Smith (New York: Basil Blackwell, 1984), 87.

13. Martin, "Play in Cats," 87.

14. Taylor, "Playing for Keeps," 271.

15. Bateson, *Steps*, 187–88.

16. Brian Sutton-Smith and Diana Kelly-Byrne, "Idealization of Play," in *Play in Animals and Humans*, ed. Peter K. Smith (New York: Basil Blackwell, 1984), 317.

17. Branigan, "Diegesis," 45.

18. André Bazin, "The Myth of Total Cinema," in *What Is Cinema?*, 2 vols., selected and translated by Hugh Gray (Berkeley: Univ. of California Press, 1971), 17–22.

19. Bazin, "Myth," 20.

20. Jerome L. Singer, *The Child's World of Make Believe: Experimental Studies of Imaginative Play* (New York: Academic Press, 1973), 195.

21. Ellis, *Why People Play*, 99–100.

8. Character

1. Neisser, *Cognition and Reality*, 77.

2. Neisser, *Cognition and Reality*, 63.

3. E. Gibson, *Principles*, 324.

4. E. Gibson, *Principles*, 326.

5. Marr, *Vision*, 24–29.

6. Ekman et al., "Universals," 712.

7. There are other studies in the literature, conducted within cultures, where there was also difficulty in distinguishing fear from surprise. The expressions of these two emotions tend to be rather similar in appearance, and their recognition is consequently highly contextually dependent. To use the terminology applied by Eleanor Rosch to the basic level of categorization, the appearance is similar, but the function is dependent upon context.

8. Ekman et al., "Universals," 713.

9. Edward E. Jones and Keith E. Davis, "From Acts to Disposi-

tions: The Attribution Process in Person Perception," in *Cognitive Theories in Social Psychology*, ed. Leonard Berkowitz (New York: Academic Press, 1978), 284.

10. Jones and Davis, "From Acts to Dispositions," 286.

11. Fritz Heider, *The Psychology of Interpersonal Relations* (New York: John Wiley, 1958). See especially 242.

12. Jones and Davis, "From Acts to Dispositions," 303.

13. The methods of science allow us to step outside the ecological envelope to obtain a god's eye view of the universe. That's why science is extraordinary, special, outside normal everyday perception.

14. For further discussion of this point see Frank P. Tomasulo, "Narrate and Describe? Point of View and Narrative Voice in *Citizen Kane*'s Thatcher Sequence," *Wide Angle* 8 (1986): 45–62.

9. Narrative

1. See Sergei Eisenstein, *Film Form*, ed. and trans. Jay Leyda (New York: Harcourt Brace, 1949), 16–17, 124.

2. Jean M. Mandler, *Stories, Scripts and Scenes: Aspects of Schema Theory* (Hillsdale, N.J.: Lawrence Erlbaum Associates, 1985), 18.

3. Mandler, *Stories*, 26.

4. Mandler, *Stories*, 47.

5. Bordwell, *Narration*, 61–62.

6. Bordwell, *Narration*, 62.

7. Neisser, "Ordinary Memory," 362.

8. Neisser, "Ordinary Memory," 363.

9. James J. Gibson, "The Problem of Event Perception," in *Reasons for Realism: Selected Essays of James J. Gibson*, ed. Edward Reed and Rebecca Jones (Hillsdale, N.J.: Lawrence Erlbaum Associates, 1982), 208.

10. Neisser, "Ordinary Memory," 364–65.

11. Branigan, *Narrative Comprehension*, 198–200.

12. Branigan, *Narrative Comprehension*, 198.

13. Marr, *Vision*, 4.

14. J. J. Gibson, *Senses*, 7.

10. Conclusion

1. Munsterberg, *The Photoplay*, 95.

2. Munsterberg, *The Photoplay*, 95.

3. The phenomenon is nested within the basic apparent motion illusion; the apparent reversal of the wagon wheels is a function of the rate at which the camera takes the series of still images and the

rate at which the wheel is turning. For example, if the camera takes a still picture twenty-four times a second and the wheel completes a revolution twenty-four times a second (or a multiple thereof) the spokes will be in exactly the same position each time the picture is taken and therefore appear to be stationary. Rotation in reverse occurs when the rate of wheel rotation (or a multiple thereof) lags slightly behind the rate of photography.

4. My account of the Arab philosopher is fictional. It was inspired, however, by my awareness of two such actual philosophers: Al-Kindi, the first philosopher of the Islamic world to undertake serious optical studies, and Alhazen, whom David Lindberg has called "the most significant figure in the history of optics between antiquity and the seventeenth century." For more information on these and other early figures in the history of visual theory, see David C. Lindberg, *Theories of Vision from Al-Kindi to Kepler* (Chicago: Univ. of Chicago Press, 1976).

5. Harry F. Harlow, "Love in Infant Monkeys," in *Frontiers of Psychological Research* (San Francisco: W. H. Freeman, 1966), 91–98.

6. Harlow, "Love," 96–97.

Selected Bibliography

Anderson, Joseph D. "An Investigation of Binocular Integration in Rivalry Phenomena." Ph.D. diss., Univ. of Iowa, 1974.

———. "Visualization and Verbalization as Mediators of Thought," *Speech Monographs* 41 (1974): 408–12.

Anderson, Joseph D., and Barbara Anderson. "Motion Perception in Motion Pictures." In *The Cinematic Apparatus,* edited by Teresa de Lauretis and Stephen Heath. New York: St. Martin's Press, 1980.

———. "The Myth of Persistence of Vision Revisited," *Journal of Film and Video,* 45,1 (Spring 1993): 3–12.

———. "Perception of the Motion Picture: An Ecological Perspective." In *Post Theory: Reconstructing Film Studies.* Edited by David Bordwell and Noel Carroll. Madison: Univ. of Wisconsin Press, forthcoming.

Anderson, Joseph D., and Barbara Fisher. "The Myth of Persistence of Vision." *Journal of the University Film Association* 30,4 (Fall 1978): 3–8.

Anderson, Joseph D. et al. "Binocular Integration in Line Rivalry," *Bulletin of the Psychonomic Society* 11,6 (1978): 399–402.

Andrew, Dudley. "Cognitivism: Quests and Questionings." *Iris* 9 (Spring 1989): 1–11.

———. *Concepts in Film Theory.* Oxford: Oxford University Press, 1984.

———. *The Major Film Theories: An Introduction.* New York: Oxford Univ. Press, 1976.

Anstis, Stuart M. "The Perception of Apparent Movement." *Philosophical Transactions of the Royal Society of London* Series B. 290: 153–168.

———. "Phi Movement as a Subtraction Process." *Vision Research* 10 (1970): 1411–30.

Armat, Thomas. "My Part in the Development of the Motion Picture Projector." Fielding, 17–22.

Arnheim, Rudolf. *Film as Art.* Berkeley: Univ. of California Press, 1966.

Atrobus, John S., ed. *Cognition and Affect*. Boston: Little, Brown and Co., 1970.

Baillargeon, Renee. "Young Infants' Physical World." *The Twelfth Annual Conference of the Cognitive Science Society*.

Barlow, Horace, Colin Blakemore, and Miranda Weston-Smith, eds. *Images and Understanding*. New York: Cambridge Univ. Press, 1990.

Bassili, John N. "Emotion Recognition: The Role of Facial Movement and the Relative Importance of Upper and Lower Areas of the Face." *Journal of Personality and Social Psychology* 37,11 (1979): 2049–58.

Bateson, Gregory. *Steps to an Ecology of Mind*. New York: Ballantine Books, 1972.

Baudry, Jean-Louis. "Ideological Effects of the Basic Cinematographic Apparatus." *Film Quarterly* 18,2 (Winter 1974/75): 39–47.

Bazin, André. "The Myth of Total Cinema." In *What is Cinema?* 2 vols. Selected and Translated by Hugh Gray. Berkeley: Univ. of California Press, 1971.

Berkowitz, Leonard, ed. *Cognitive Theories in Social Psychology*. New York: Academic Press, 1978.

Bickhard, Mark H., and D. Michael Richie. *On the Nature of Representation*. New York: Praeger, 1983.

Biederman, Irving. "Recognition-by-Components: A Theory of Human Image Understanding." *Psychological Review* 94,2 (1987): 115–47.

Biederman-Thorson, Marguerite, John Thorson, and G. David Lange. "Apparent Movement Due to Closely Spaced Sequentially Flashed Dots in the Human Peripheral Field of Vision." *Vision Research* 11 (1971): 889–903.

Boff, Kenneth R., Lloyd Kaufman, and James Thomas, eds. *Handbook of Perception and Human Performance*. New York: John Wiley, 1986.

Bordwell, David. "A Case for Cognitivism." *Iris* 9 (Spring 1989): 11–41.

———. *Making Meaning: Inference and Rhetoric in the Interpretation of Cinema*. Cambridge: Harvard Univ. Press, 1989.

———. *Narration in the Fiction Film*. Madison: Univ. of Wisconsin Press, 1985.

Bordwell, David, and Kristin Thompson. *Film Art: An Introduction*. Reading, MA: Addison and Wesley, 1979.

Boring, Edwin S. *Sensation and Perception in the History of Experimental Psychology*. New York: Appleton-Century-Crofts, 1942.

Boynton, Robert M. *Human Color Vision*. New York: Holt, Rinehart and Winston, 1979.

Braddick, Oliver J. "The Masking of Apparent Motion in Random Dot Patterns." *Vision Research* 13 (1973): 355–69.

———. "A Short Range Process in Apparent Motion." *Vision Research* 14 (1974): 519–26.

Braddick, Oliver J., and A. J. Allard. "Apparent Motion and the Motion Detector." In *Visual Psychophysics and Physiology*, edited by J. Armington, J. Krausskopf, and B. R. Wooten. New York: Academic Press, 1978.

Branigan, Edward. "Diegesis and Authorship in Film." *Iris* 7,4 (Fall 1986): 37–54.

———. *Narrative Comprehension and Film*. New York: Routledge, Chapman and Hall, 1992.

———. *Point of View in the Cinema: A Theory of Narration and Subjectivity in Classical Film*. Hawthorne, NY: Mouton, 1984.

Braunstein, Myron L., and James S. Tittle. "The Observer-Relative Velocity Field as the Basis for Effective Motion Parallax." *Journal of Experimental Psychology: Human Perception and Performance* 14,4 (1988): 582–90.

Bregman, Albert S. *Auditory Scene Analysis*. Cambridge: MIT Press, 1990.

Breitmeyer, Bruno, Rhonda Love, and Barry Wepman. "Contour Suppression During Stroboscopic Motion and Metacontrast." *Vision Research* 14 (1974): 1451–56.

Brooks, Virginia. "Film, Perception and Cognitive Psychology." *Millenium Film Journal* 14/15 (1984): 105–26.

———. "Restoring the Meaning in Cinematic Movement: What is the Text in a Dance Film?" *Iris* 9 (Spring 1989): 69–105.

Bruce, Vicki. *Recognizing Faces*. Hillsdale, N.J.: Lawrence Erlbaum Associates, 1988.

Bruce, Vicki, and Patrick R. Green. *Visual Perception: Physiology, Psychology and Ecology*. 2d ed. Hillsdale, N.J.: Lawrence Erlbaum Associates, 1990.

Carroll, John M., and T. G. Bever. "Segmentation in Cinema Perception." *Science* 191 (12 Mar. 1976): 1053–55.

Carroll, Noel. *Mystifying Movies*. New York: Columbia Univ. Press, 1988.

———. *Philosophical Problems in Classical Film Theory*. Princeton: Princeton Univ. Press, 1988.

———. "The Power of Movies." *Daedalus* 114,4 (Fall 1985): 79–103.

————. "Toward a Theory of Point of View Editing." *Poetics Today* 14,1 (Spring 1993): 123–41.

Carterette, Edward C., and Morton P. Friedman, eds. *Handbook of Perception*. Vol. 10, *Perceptual Ecology*. New York: Academic Press, 1978.

Chomsky, Noam. *Knowledge of Language: Its Nature, Origin and Use.* New York: Praeger, 1986.

Churchland, Patricia S., and Terrence J. Sejnowski. "Perspectives on Cognitive Neuroscience." *Science* 242 (4 Nov. 1988): 741–45.

Clynes, Manfred. *Sentics: The Touch of Emotion*. New York: Doubleday, 1977.

Collins, W. Andrew. "Recent Advances in Research on Cognitive Processing Television Viewing." *Journal of Broadcasting* 25,4 (Fall 1981): 327–35.

Crozier, W. Ray, and Anthony J. Chapman, eds. *Cognitive Processes in the Perception of Art*. Netherlands: Elsevier Science Publishers, 1984.

Cutting, James E. *Perception with an Eye for Motion*. Cambridge: MIT Press, 1986.

————. "Perceptual Artifacts and Phenomena: Gibson's Role in the 20th Century." In *Foundations of Perceptual Theory*, edited by Sergio C. Masin, 231–60. Amsterdam: Elsevier Science Publishers, 1993.

————. "Rigidity in Cinema Seen from the Front Row, Side Aisle." *Journal of Experimental Psychology: Human Perception and Performance* 13,3 (1987): 323–34.

Darwin, Charles. *On the Origin of Species*. Facsimile ed. Cambridge: Harvard Univ. Press, 1964.

Deregowski, Jan. "Geometric Restitution of Perspective: Bartel's Method." *Perception* 18,5 (1989): 595–600.

Deregowski, J. B., and A. M. Bentley. "Seeing the Impossible and Building the Likely." *British Journal of Psychology* 78 (1987): 91–97.

Dewey, John. *Art as Experience*. New York: G. P. Putnam's Sons, 1958.

Diamond, Adele. "The Planning, Execution and Inhibition of Movement During Infancy." *The Twelfth Annual Conference of the Cognitive Science Society*.

Dick, Miri, Shimon Ullman, and Dov Sagi. "Parallel and Serial Processes in Motion Detection." *Science* 237 (July 1987): 400–402.

Dooling, Robert J., and Stewart H. Hulse, eds. *The Comparative Psy-*

chology of Audition. Hillsdale, N.J.: Lawrence Erlbaum Associates, 1989.

Eibl-Eibesfeldt, Irenaus. *Ethology: The Biology of Behavior*. New York: Holt, Rinehart and Winston, 1970.

Eisenstein, Sergei M. *Film Essays and a Lecture*. Edited and translated by Jay Leyda. New York: Praeger, 1970.

———. *Film Form*. Edited and translated by Jay Leyda. New York: Harcourt Brace, 1949.

———. *The Film Sense*. Edited and translated by Jay Leyda. New York: Harcourt Brace, 1942.

———. *Nonindifferent Nature*. Cambridge: Cambridge Univ. Press, 1987.

———. *Selected Works: Writings, 1922–1934*. Bloomington: Indiana Univ. Press, 1987.

Ekman, Paul, and Wallace V. Friesen. *Unmasking the Face*. Englewood Cliffs, N.J.: Prentice-Hall, 1975.

Ekman, Paul, Robert W. Levenson, and Wallace V. Friesen. "Autonomic Nervous System Activity Distinguishes Among Emotions." *Science* 221 (16 Sept. 1983): 1208–10.

Ekman, Paul, and Maureen O'Sullivan. "The Role of Context in Interpreting Facial Expression." *Journal of Experimental Psychology: General* 117,1 (1988): 86–88.

Ekman, Paul, et al. "Universals and Cultural Differences in the Judgments of Facial Expressions of Emotion." *Journal of Personality and Social Psychology* 53,4 (1987): 712–17.

Ellis, Michael J. *Why People Play*. Englewood Cliffs, N.J.: Prentice-Hall, 1973.

Estes, W. K. ed., *Human Information Processing*. Vol. 5, *Handbook of Learning and Cognitive Processes*. Hillsdale, N.J.: Lawrence Erlbaum Associates, 1978.

Evans, James R., and Manfred Clynes, eds. *Rhythm in Psychological, Linguistic and Musical Processes*. Springfield: Charles C. Thomas, 1986.

Eysenck, Michael W., ed. *Cognitive Psychology: An International Review*. New York: John Wiley, 1990.

Fielding, Raymond. "Accounting Practices in the Early American Motion Picture Industry." *Historical Journal of Film, Radio and Television* 12,2 (1992): 115–25.

Fielding, Raymond, ed. *A Technological History of Motion Pictures and Television*. Berkeley: Univ. of California Press, 1967.

Fodor, Jerry A. *Modularity of Mind.* Cambridge: MIT Press, 1983.

Fodor, Jerry A., and Zenon W. Pylyshyn. "How Direct is Visual Perception?" *Cognition* 9 (1981): 139–96.

Freeman, Walter J. "The Physiology of Perception." *Scientific American* 264,2 (Feb. 1991): 78–85.

Freyd, Jennifer J. "Dynamic Mental Representations." *Psychological Review* 94,4 (1987): 427–38.

Gardner, Howard. *The Mind's New Science: A History of the Cognitive Revolution.* New York: Basic Books, 1985.

Gazzaniga, Michael S. *Mind Matters.* Boston: Houghton Mifflin, 1989.

———. *Nature's Mind: The Biological Roots of Thinking, Emotions, Sexuality, Language and Intelligence.* New York: Basic Books, 1992.

———. *The Social Brain: Discovering the Networks of the Mind.* New York: Basic Books, 1985.

Gibson, Eleanor J. *Principles of Perceptual Learning and Development.* Englewood Cliffs, N.J.: Prentice-Hall, 1969.

Gibson, Eleanor J., ed. *An Odyssey in Learning and Perception.* Cambridge: MIT Press, 1991.

Gibson, James J. *The Ecological Approach to Visual Perception.* Boston: Houghton Mifflin, 1979.

———. "Perception as a Function of Stimulation." in *Psychology: A Study of Science.* Vol. 1, edited by S. Koch. New York: McGraw-Hill, 1959.

———. *The Perception of the Visual World.* Boston: Houghton Mifflin, 1950.

———. "The Problem of Event Perception." In *Reasons for Realism: Selected Essays of James J. Gibson,* edited by Edward Reed and Rebecca Jones. Hillsdale, N.J.: Lawrence Erlbaum Associates, 1982.

———. *Reasons for Realism.* Edited by Edward Reed and Rebecca Jones. Hillsdale, N.J.: Lawrence Erlbaum Associates, 1982.

———. *The Senses Considered as Perceptual Systems.* Boston: Houghton Mifflin, 1966.

Gombrich, Ernst H. *Art And Illusion: A Study in the Psychology of Pictorial Representation.* Princeton: Princeton Univ. Press, 1960.

———. "Illusion and Art." In *Illusion in Nature and Art.* Edited by R. L. Gregory and E. H. Gombrich. London: Duckworth, 1973.

———. *The Image and the Eye: Further Studies in the Psychology of Pictorial Representation.* Ithaca: Cornell Univ. Press, 1982.

———. "Representation and Misrepresentation." *Critical Inquiry* 11,2 (Dec. 1984): 195–201.

———. "The What and the How: Perspective Representation and the Phenomenal World." In *Logic and Art: Essays in Honor of Nelson Goodman*, edited by Richard Rudner and Israel Scheffler. Indianapolis: Bobbs-Merrill Co., 1972.

Gregory, Richard L. *The Intelligent Eye*. New York: McGraw-Hill, 1970.

Gregory, Richard L., and E. H. Gombrich, eds. *Illusion in Nature and Art*. New York: Charles Scribner's Sons, 1973.

Hamilton, Vernon, Gordon H. Bower, and Nico Frijda, eds. *Cognitive Perspectives on Emotion and Motivation*. Netherlands: Kluwer Academic Publishers, 1988.

Harlow, Harry F. "Love in Infant Monkeys." In *Frontiers of Psychological Research*, selected by Stanley Coopersmith. San Francisco: W. H. Freeman, 1966.

Heider, Fritz. *The Psychology of Interpersonal Relations*. New York: John Wiley, 1958.

Hewstone, Miles, ed. *Attribution Theory*. Oxford: Basil Blackwell, 1983.

Hochberg, Julian, "Gestalt Theory." In *The Oxford Companion to the Mind*, edited by Richard L. Gregory. Oxford: Oxford Univ. Press, 1987.

———. *Perception* . New York: Prentice-Hall, 1978.

———. "The Perception of Moving Images." *Iris* 9 (Spring 1989): 41–69.

———. "Piecemeal Organization and Cognitive Components in Object Perception: Perceptually Coupled Responses to Moving Objects." *Journal of Experimental Psychology: General* 116,4 (1987): 370–80.

Hubel, David H., and Torsten N. Wiesel. "Brain Mechanisms of Vision." In *The Mind's Eye*, edited by Jeremy M. Wolfe. New York: W. H. Freeman, 1986.

———. "Receptive Fields, Binocular Interaction, and Functional Architecture in the Cat's Visual Cortex." *Journal of Physiology* 160 (1962): 106–54.

Hummel, John E., and Irving Biederman. "Dynamic Binding: A Basis for the Representation of Shape by Neural Networks." In *The Twelfth Annual Conference of the Cognitive Science Society*. Hillsdale, N.J.: Lawrence Erlbaum Associates, 1990.

———. "Dynamic Binding in a Neural Network for Shape Recognition." Unpublished manuscript, Dept. of Psychology, Univ. of Minnesota.

Humphreys, Glyn, and Vicki Bruce. *Visual Cognition*. Hillsdale, N.J.: Lawrence Erlbaum Associates, 1989.

Hurvich, Leo M., and Dorthea Jameson. "An Opponent Process Theory of Color Vision." *Psychological Review* 64 (1957): 384–404.

———. "Opponent Processes as a Model of Neural Organization." *American Psychologist* 29 (1974): 88–102.

———. *The Perception of Brightness and Darkness.* Boston: Allyn and Bacon, 1966.

Izard, Carroll E. *The Face of Emotion.* New York: Appleton-Century-Crofts, 1971.

Jensen, A. G. "The Evolution of Modern Television." Fielding, 235–249.

Jones, Edward E. *Attribution: Perceiving the Causes of Behavior.* Morristown, N.J.: General Learning Corporation, 1972.

Jones, Edward E., and Keith E. Davis. "From Acts to Dispositions: The Attribution Process in Person Perception." In *Cognitive Theories in Social Psychology,* edited by Leonard Berkowitz. New York: Academic Press, 1978.

Jose, Paul E., and William F. Brewer. "Development of Story Liking: Character Identification, Suspense, and Outcome Resolution." *Developmental Psychology* 20,5 (1984): 911–24.

Julesz, Bela. *Foundations of Cyclopean Perception.* Chicago: Univ. of Chicago Press, 1971.

Kaufman, Lloyd. *Sight and Mind: an Introduction to Visual Perception.* New York: Oxford Univ. Press, 1974.

Kellogg, Edward W. "History of Sound Motion Pictures." Fielding, 174–220.

Kennedy, John M. *A Psychology of Picture Perception.* San Francisco: Jossey-Bass, 1974.

Kintsch, W., J. Miller, and P. Polson, eds. *Methods and Tactics in Cognitive Science.* Hillsdale, N.J.: Lawrence Erlbaum Associates, 1984.

Koch, Sigmund, and David E. Leary, eds. *A Century of Psychology as Science.* New York: McGraw Hill, 1985.

Kolers, Paul A. *Aspects of Motion Perception.* International Series of Monographs in Experimental Psychology, vol. 16. Oxford: Pergamon Press, 1972.

Koste, Virgina G. *Dramatic Play in Childhood: Rehearsal for Life.* New Orleans: Anchorage Press, 1978.

Kracauer, Siegfried. *Theory of Film: The Redemption of Physical Reality.* New York: Oxford Univ. Press, 1960.

Krieger, Murray. "The Ambiguities of Respresentation and Illusion:

An E. H. Gombrich Retrospective." *Critical Inquiry* 11,2 (1984): 181–84.

Kuleshov, Lev. *Kuleshov on Film.* Translated and edited by Ronald Levaco. Berkeley: Univ. of California Press, 1974.

Kulikowski, J. J., and D. J. Tolhurst. "Psychophysical Evidence for Sustained and Transient Detectors in Human Vision." *Journal of Physiology* 232 (1973): 149–62.

Lakoff, George. *Women, Fire, and Dangerous Things: What Categories Reveal about the Mind.* Chicago: Univ. of Chicago Press, 1987.

Lamarck, Jean Baptiste Pierre Antoine de Monet de. *Philosophie zoologique.* Paris: Dentu, 1809; Weinheim: H. R. Englemann, 1960.

Land, Edwin H. "Our 'Polar Partnership' with the World Around Us." *Harvard Magazine* 80,3 (Jan.-Feb. 1978): 23–26.

———. "Recent Advances in Retinex Theory." *Vision Research* 26,1 (1986): 7–21.

———. "The Retinex Theory of Color Vision." *Scientific American* 237,6 (Dec. 1977): 108–29.

Lieberman, Nina J. *Playfulness: Its Relationship to Imagination and Creativity.* New York: Academic Press, 1977.

Lindberg, David C. *Theories of Vision from Al-Kindi to Kepler.* Chicago: Univ. of Chicago Press, 1976.

Livingstone, Margaret S. "Art, Illusion and the Visual System." *Scientific American* 258,1 (Jan. 1988): 78–85.

Livingstone, Margaret S., and David H. Hubel. "Segregation of Form, Color, Movement, and Depth: Anatomy, Physiology and Perception." *Science* 240 (6 May 1988): 740–49.

MacLeod, Robert B., and Herbert L. Pick, Jr., eds. *Perception: Essays in Honor of James J. Gibson.* Ithaca: Cornell Univ. Press, 1974.

Mandler, Jean M. *Stories, Scripts and Scenes: Aspects of Schema Theory.* Hillsdale, N.J.: Lawrence Erlbaum Associates, 1984.

Mandler, Jean, and Nancy Johnson. "Remembrance of Things Parsed: Story, Structure, and Recall." *Cognitive Psychology* 9 (1977): 111–51.

Marks, Lawrence E. *The Unity of the Senses: Interrelations among the Modalities.* New York: Academic Press, 1978.

Marr, David. *Vision.* New York: W. H. Freeman, 1982.

Martin, Paul. "The Whys and Wherefores of Play in Cats." Smith, 71–94.

Masin, Sergio C., ed. *Foundations of Perceptual Theory.* Advances in

Psychology, vol. 99. Amsterdam: Elsevier Science Publishers, 1993.

Massaro, Dominic W. *Speech Perception by Eye and Ear: A Paradigm for Psychological Inquiry.* Hillsdale, N.J.: Lawrence Erlbaum Associates, 1987.

Mast, Gerald, and Marshall Cohen, eds. *Film Theory and Criticism: Introductory Readings.* New York: Oxford Univ. Press, 1979.

Mayer, Ernst. "Evolution." *Scientific American* 239,3 (Sept. 1978): 46–56.

Metz, Christian. *Film Language.* New York: Oxford Univ. Press, 1974.

Meyer, Leonard B. *Emotion and Meaning in Music.* Chicago: Univ. of Chicago Press, 1956.

Michaels, Claire F., and Claudia Carello. *Direct Perception.* Englewood Cliffs, N.J.: Prentice-Hall, 1981.

Michalos, Alexandros C., ed. *Philosphical Problems of Science and Technology.* Boston: Allyn and Bacon, 1974.

Milner, Peter M. *Physiological Psychology.* New York: Holt, Rinehart and Winston, 1970.

Moore, Brian C. J. *An Introduction to the Psychology of Hearing.* New York: Academic Press, 1989.

Munsterberg, Hugo. *The Photoplay: A Psychological Study.* New York: D. Appleton, 1916. Reprint, *The Film: A Psychological Study,* New York: Dover Publications, 1970.

———. "Why we Go to the 'Movies'," *Cosmopolitan,* 15 Dec. 1915, 22–32.

Munsterberg, Margaret. *Hugo Munsterberg: His Life and Work.* New York: Appleton, 1922.

Nakayama, Ken. "Visual Inference in the Perception of Occluded Surfaces." *The Twelfth Annual Conference of the Cognitive Science Society.*

Narmour, Eugene. *The Analysis and Cognition of Basic Melodic Structures.* Chicago: Univ. of Chicago Press, 1990.

Neisser, Ulric. *Cognition and Reality.* New York: W. H. Freeman, 1976.

———. "From Direct Perception to Conceptual Structure." In *Concepts and Conceptual Development,* edited by Ulric Neisser. Cambridge: Cambridge Univ. Press, 1987.

———. "Interpreting Harry Bahrick's Discovery: What Confers Immunity Against Forgetting?" *Journal of Experimental Psychology: General* 113,1 (1984): 32–35.

————. "The Role of Theory in the Ecological Study of Memory." *Journal of Experimental Psycholoy: General* 114,2 (1985): 272–76.

————. "What is Ordinary Memory the Memory Of?" In *Remembering Reconsidered*, edited by Ulric Neisser and Eugene Winograd. Cambridge: Cambridge Univ. Press, 1988.

Neisser, Ulric, ed. *Concepts and Conceptual Development*. Cambridge: Cambridge Univ. Press, 1987.

Neisser, Ulric, and Eugene Winograd, eds. *Remembering Reconsidered*. Cambridge: Cambridge Univ. Press, 1988.

Nell, Victor. *Lost in a Book: The Psychology of Reading for Pleasure*. New Haven: Yale Univ. Press, 1988.

Nizhny, Vladimir. *Lessons with Eisenstein*. Edited and translated by Ivor Montagu and Jay Leyda. New York: Hill and Wang, 1962.

O'Connor, N., and B. Hermelin. "Coding Strategies of Normal and Handicapped Children." In *Intersensory Perception and Sensory Integration*, edited by R. D. Walk and H. L. Pick, 315–43. New York: Plenum, 1981.

Osherson, Daniel N., and Edward E. Smith, eds. *Thinking*. Vol. 3, *An Invitation to Cognitive Science*. Cambridge: MIT Press, 1990.

Osherson, D. N., S. M. Kosslyn, and J. M. Hollerbach, eds. *Visual Cognition and Action*. Vol 2, *An Invitation to Cognitive Science*. Cambridge: MIT Press, 1990.

Panofsky, Erwin. "Perspective as Symbolic Form." Translation of "Die Perspektive als symbolische Form" (Vortrage de Bibliothek, Warburg, vol. 4, 1924–25, p. 258–330.) Photocopy of typescript, 18.

Petersik, J. Timothy. "The Two-Process Distinction in Apparent Motion." *Psychological Bulletin* 106,1 (1989): 107–27.

Pick Anne D., ed. *Perception and Its Development: A Tribute to Eleanor J. Gibson*. Hillsdale, N.J.: Lawrence Erlbaum Associates, 1979.

Pinker, Steven, ed. *Visual Cognition*. Cambridge: MIT Press, 1985.

Plutchik, Robert. *Emotion: A Psychoevolutionary Synthesis*. New York: Harper and Row, 1980.

Popper, Karl R. "Truth, Rationality, and the Growth of Scientific Knowledge." In *Philosophical Problems of Science and Technology*, edited by Alexandros C. Michalos. Boston: Allyn and Bacon, 1974.

Proffitt, Dennis R. "A Hierarchical Approach to Perception." In *Foundations of Perceptual Theory*. Vol. 99, *Advances in Psychology*, edited by Sergio C. Masin. Amsterdam: Elsevier Science Publishers, 1993.

Pudovkin, V. I. *Film Technique and Film Acting*. Translated by Ivor Montagu. New York: Grove Press, 1960.

Ramachandran, Vilayanur S., and Stuart M. Anstis. "The Perception of Apparent Motion." *Scientific American* 254,6 (June 1986): 102–9.

Reed, Edward S. *James J. Gibson and the Psychology of Perception*. New Haven: Yale Univ. Press, 1988.

Rennie, John. "DNA's New Twists." *Scientific American* 26,3 (Mar. 1993): 122–32.

Rock, Irvin. *An Introduction to Perception*. New York: Macmillan, 1975.

———. *The Logic of Perception*. Cambridge: MIT Press, 1983.

———. *Perception* . New York: Scientific American Library, 1984.

Shultz, Thomas R. "Play as Arousal Modulation." In *Play and Learning*, edited by Brian Sutton-Smith. New York: Gardner Press, 1979.

Singer, Jerome L. *The Child's World of Make Believe: Experimental Studies of Imaginative Play*. New York: Academic Press, 1973.

Small, Edward S., and Joseph D. Anderson. "What's in a Flicker Film?" *Communication Monographs* 43,1 (Mar. 1976).

Smets, G. J. F., C. J. Overbeeke, and M. H. Stratmann. "Depth on a Flat Screen." *Perceptual and Motor Skills* 64 (1987): 1023–34.

Smith, Peter K., ed. *Play in Animals and Humans*. New York: Basil Blackwell, 1984.

Spelke, Elizabeth S. "Exploring Audible and Visible Events in Infancy." In *Perception and its Development*, edited by Anne D. Pick. Hillsdale, N.J.: Lawrence Erlbaum Associates, 1979.

Spence, Janet T., and Carrol E. Izard, eds. *Motivation, Emotion, and Personality*. Amsterdam: Elsevier Science Publishers, 1985.

Sperling, George, Michael S. Landy, Barbara A. Dosher, and Mark E. Perkins. "Kinetic Depth Effect and Identification of Shape." *Journal of Experimental Psychology: Human Perception and Performance* 15,4 (1989): 826–40.

Steiner, Wendy, ed. *Image and Code*. Ann Arbor: Univ. of Michigan, 1981.

Sutton-Smith, Brian, ed. *Play and Learning*. New York: Gardner Press, 1979.

Sutton-Smith, Brian, and Diane Kelly-Byrne. "Idealization of Play." Smith, 305–321.

Taylor, Sue Parker. "Playing for Keeps." Smith, 271–293.

Tomasulo, Frank P. "Narrate and Describe? Point of View and Narrative Voice in *Citizen Kane's* Thatcher Sequence." *Wide Angle* 8 (1986): 45–62.

The Twelfth Annual Conference of the Cognitive Science Society. Hillsdale, N.J.: Lawrence Erlbaum Associates, 1990.

Ullman, Shiman. "Against Direct Perception." *The Behavioral and Brain Sciences* 3 (1980): 373–81.

Vygotsky, L. S. *Mind in Society: The Development of Higher Psychological Processes.* Cambridge: Harvard Univ. Press, 1978.

Walk, Richard D., and Herbert L. Pick, Jr., eds. *Intersensory Perception and Sensory Integration.* New York: Plenum Press, 1981.

Wertheimer, Max. "Experimental Studies on the Seeing of Motion." In *Classics in Psychology,* edited by Thorne Shipley. New York: Philosophical Library, 1961.

Young, Andrew W., and Hadyn D. Ellis, eds. *Handbook of Research on Face Processing.* Amsterdam: Elsevier Science Publishers, 1989.

Zajonc, R. B. "On the Primacy of Affect." *American Psychologist* 39,2 (Feb. 1984): 117–23.

Zeki, Semir. "The Visual Image in Mind and Brain." *Scientific American* 267,3 (Sept. 1992): 69–76.

Index

Joseph D. Anderson teaches motion picture production and theory in the Department of Theatre and Film at the University of Kansas, where he heads the Institute for Cognitive Studies in Film and Video. He holds a Ph.D. in film studies and perceptual psychology from the University of Iowa. He has conducted laboratory research in visual perception at the University of Wisconsin and spent more than a dozen years working in the motion picture industry.